THE uTOPIA SERIES

LOCAL MOTION

The Art of Civic Engagement in Toronto

Edited by Dave Meslin, Christina Palassio, Alana Wilcox

Coach House Books, Toronto

First edition

 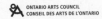

Published with the generous assistance of the Canada Council for the Arts
and the Ontario Arts Council. Coach House Books also gratefully acknowl-
edges the support of the Government of Ontario through the Ontario Book
Publishing Tax Credit and the Ontario Media Development Corporation's
Book Fund, as well as the Government of Canada through the Canada
Book Fund.

The opinions expressed in these essays do not necessarily reflect those
of the editors or Coach House Books.

Library and Archives Canada Cataloguing in Publication

Local motion : the art of civic engagement in Toronto / edited by Dave
Meslin, Christina Palassio, Alana Wilcox.

(The UTOpia series)
ISBN 978-1-55245-238-7

1. Political participation–Ontario–Toronto.
2. Toronto (Ont.)–Politics and government.
3. Municipal government–Ontario–Toronto–Citizen participation I. Meslin,
Dave II. Palassio, Christina III. Wilcox, Alana IV. Series: UTOpia series

JS211.L63 2010   323'.04209713541   C2010-907050-X

Table of Contents

Foreword
Dionne Brand

This is a remarkable city when one considers all the gifts its multicultural multitudes present. Yet its politicians are gloomy about its future, if their dire rhetoric is to be believed. They imagine it as a bloated and corpulent society in need of reining in. They describe a city in which the needs of people are excessive and unreasonable. Some suggest our problems lie in too many of the wrong sort of people: illegals – laughably raising the spectre of illegal bodies to a citizenry of immigrants. They tell us less public transit is better, fewer schools are better, fewer teachers are better and even less political representation is better. These solutions, in a city growing more populous and cosmopolitan by the second. George Orwell said, in a 1945 essay, that, in literary works, favourable utopias seemed alike in postulating perfection while being unable to suggest happiness. I'm struck by how apt Orwell's description is for the views of our municipal politicians. Cuts to every social good seem to be their idea of perfection. Happiness is another matter.

Wary of sounding apocalyptic myself, I find Toronto in a standoff, the standoff between those who run it and those who live in it. There is a failure of those who rule to truly acknowledge those who live in the city as anything more than the projections of their own fears. Orwell describes the representation of happiness in literary utopias as boring and desultory, but our politicians don't even offer us visions of a boring and desultory happiness; they do not even offer us relief from hardship and, in fact, they earnestly promise us *more* hardship.

The future seems strikingly unavailable to our politicians – they are all in a holding pattern. None even bother to fabricate a decent lie of a utopia, none even have the sincere but mad imagination of, say, Margaret Atwood's Crake, and none are as daring or ordinary as her Gardeners. Instead they are militant in their embrace of a restricting, distressing future of nothing.

There is a city here waiting to be imagined. I know. There must be, because I see it each time I walk out of my house. I was affected by a detail of the September 2010 fire in St. James Town. Police found more that two hundred 'canary like' birds in one apartment. Now I know this story will turn out badly, for they say the birds were in poor condition; and it may be that the bird keeper was keeping birds for sale and in all probability it is all illegal and tawdry. But I prefer to read this lacuna into the life of the city differently. Someone came home each day to two hundred or more birds, someone lived in an apartment surrounded by two hundred birds – a small apartment in a maze of small apartments, in a maze of apartment buildings in downtown Toronto, with the city outside bustling, noisy, hot, cold, amid the travails and anxiety of subway and streetcar, construction and sirens – that's vision. I'd like to vote for someone with that kind of imagination.

I tell my youngest sister about this person and she tells me, Oh, that's not unusual. She happens to know a guy who raised birds, hundreds, in his basement in Scarborough. He fed them different-coloured dyes in their food so their feathers would turn those colours, she says. Are you kidding me, I ask. No, no, she replies, his wife got fed up with the noise though, so now he collects electronics. Then there was a family in the downtown who grew a fig tree every summer only to dig it up and bury it for the winter and then replant it to grow again the next summer. All for the brief possibility of a few fresh figs. So the person in St. James Town is not unique. Well, I think that's even more astonishing. It looks like there are eruptions of imagination all over the city.

And that's what this book is for. The imaginations of our politicians are bankrupt. And, as Orwell also said, it's not that we want 'some central-heated, air-conditioned, strip-lighted Paradise ... " But a city with an imagination for birds and fig trees is a beginning step, and one many of us are willing to imagine into being. The city, after all, belongs to us.

Dionne Brand is the Poet Laureate of the City of Toronto. She has written nine volumes of poetry and four works of fiction. For her poetry she has received the Governor General's Award, the Pat Lowther Award and the Trillium Book Award, and for her fiction she has received the Toronto Book Award. She is also Professor of English in the School of English and Theatre Studies at the University of Guelph.

Introduction
Dave Meslin, Christina Palassio, Alana Wilcox

As this book goes to press, Toronto finds itself in the throes of a municipal election. The pages of this book are being printed, folded and glued together as voters cast ballots that will determine the political leadership of the city for the next four years. The timing is not a coincidence: the premise of this book is that civic engagement shouldn't start and end on election day. We often get so wrapped up in election coverage and the celebrification of politics that we forget that cities are shaped by the people who live in them. Voting for and electing a city council is just one step in participating in civic life; after we elect our mayor and members of Council, we need to find a way to work together to build the city we want.

When we think about politics, we often think of provincial or federal issues: health care, gun control or foreign aid. But the local level is where we can have the greatest impact, because the municipal government is more accessible, tangible and immediately relevant than its provincial or federal counterparts. City Hall is where decisions about roads, parks, schools, transit and planning are made. Municipal politicians are more available and approachable than their colleagues at the province and in Ottawa and, without the presence of official party structures, City Hall operates in a much more organic and intuitive way than other levels of government, which means it's a natural starting point for political engagement. Few politicians, however, know how to truly inspire, to shift the political landscape to create new opportunities: most simply operate in the narrow space between the goalposts of existing norms. Real change is most often driven by ordinary people who are stubborn, passionate and motivated.

One thing that has troubled us the most during the run-up to this municipal election is the shift of vocabulary: in much of the campaign-speak, we are no longer 'citizens' but 'taxpayers.' This is an unfortunate word because it limits the role we play. Our relationship to the city is not purely financial. We're not here as customers. We're here as neighbours and families. In other words, we don't just pay for the city, we live in it, and we care about the shape it takes and how that affects our lives.

In fact, we think that the word 'citizen,' while it automatically entitles us to certain basic rights and privileges, also demands something in exchange. What your city can do for you is important; the flip side, what you can do for your city, is the other half of the deal. It needn't be as extravagant as building a hospital: you can organize a neighbourhood picnic, fight the demolition of a beautiful building, run for City Council, even just pick up some litter. We can't wait for the politicians to do these things for us. The way to make our city better is to do it ourselves.

The first five books of the *uTOpia* series looked at great ideas for Toronto, giving voice to bold and creative proposals about culture, the environment, water and food. In these books, contributors talked about creating a Children's Council, a legal place for street art, a better Brick Works, spaces for community-driven plans for Toronto's waterfront and urban farms. In *Local Motion*, we shift the focus from the 'what' to the 'how.' We examine some of the ways our city doesn't work: Ed Keenan looks at the flaws in our electoral system and how they might be reformed, and Denise Balkissoon considers how we might make City Hall more representative of our diversity. We also explore the lives and stories of Toronto's city-builders, who show what it means to be civically engaged. Hannah Sung writes about how Tamara Dawit uses music to empower incarcerated youth. John Lorinc profiles Nick Pierre, who worked with Council and the City to build a skate park in his East York neighbourhood. And Catherine Porter talks to the indomitable Jutta Mason, whose efforts at Dufferin Grove Park, sometimes perpetrated under cover of night, are often cited as an example of the best civic engagement can accomplish. Each of the stories in the book is unique, but common themes emerge: change is collaborative, change requires patience, and to effect change, you have to know how the system works. We offer some help on that front, including tips for navigating the bureaucracy (with great illustrations by Marlena Zuber), and from-the-trenches advice from Jennifer Lewington on winning over the media. Inspiring examples and practical tips give you tools and information you can use to start changing your community for the better.

The most vital ingredient for a healthy, beautiful, creative and prosperous city is strong civic participation. The strength of a city lies not in the corridors of its City Hall, but in its neighbourhoods, where the collective wisdom and passion of its residents transforms ideas and dreams into projects and campaigns. This book profiles community leaders and their projects in the hopes of putting a human face on leadership and perhaps creating in you, the reader, a spark of curiosity to explore your own inner activist.

Bert Archer

Teaching the City of No to say yes

Saying no is easier than saying yes. Saying no requires no follow-up. No means no. Yes implies further discussion, complications. Yes means any number of things.

Toronto is a city of no. Municipal activists in many cities rally around no. The yeses, for some reason, tend to be limited to the more frolicsome end of the spectrum: artistic interventions, with guerrilla gardening escapades like Eric Cheung and Sean Martindale's efforts to turn poster hoardings into planters, or Newmindspace's Yonge-Dundas Square pillow fights and those TTC be-ins that happen from time to time. All charming, but none as substantial as our resoundingly productive no's, such as the Spadina Expressway, or saving Old City Hall from the Eatons, or Trefann Court. Our no's are big, serious, adult. Why aren't our yeses?

Human nature plays a part.

I spent the summer of 2006 attending public meetings and turning them into weekly columns for the *Globe and Mail*'s Toronto section. I went to at least one and sometimes several meetings around the city every week, where things like condo towers and women's shelters, big-box stores and dog parks were discussed. In all, I went to a couple dozen of those public meetings. Two of them stand out especially.

The first one was attended by three people other than me and the city councillor: a woman, her husband and their baby. They wanted a speed bump put in on their block, Carmichael Avenue between Bathurst and Falkirk, where, they said, more than thirty children lived. They didn't get it, as far as I know. But that little meeting ended up being the only one of those more than twenty that was based on people's wanting to add something to the neighbourhood, rather than wanting to remove something or keep it out.

But it's the other public meeting that really distilled the no-ness of the most basic forms of municipal activism, as well as that no-ness's roots in some fundamentally self-regarding aspects of human nature. It was in the Kingsway, Toronto's first planned community. It's like every residential neighbourhood, but more so. People move to the Kingsway because they like the way it is. They like the long, low front lawns, their proto-ranch-style bunga-lows or their mock-Tudor two-storey detacheds. And they like the sort of people who like those things, too, and like living among them. So when the Butorac family moved in, a couple in their thir-ties with, I think, two young children, this community of mostly fifty- and sixty-somethings didn't take kindly to their way of doing things; specifically, their putting a fence around their front yard to give their backyardless corner lot a sanctuary for the kids to play.

Those most opposed came to a public meeting, presided over by their city councillor, Peter Milczyn, to confront the Butoracs. Their neighbourhood was not the sort of neighbourhood that had front-yard fences, they said. Over the course of about an hour, they browbeat the Butoracs, who said they had already spent more than $10,000 putting up a fence, and another several thousand taking it down, into planting a hedge instead. The Butoracs had paid more than a million dollars for their home, and they wanted a fence. But their neighbours didn't, so they said no.

Groups of concerned neighbours, often in the form of ratepayers' associations, tend in practice to get set up in opposi-tion to something, and they only really reactivate when there's something else to stop. The Annex Residents' Association, for example, seems to exist primarily to give people an outlet to oppose home renovations they don't think are Annexy enough. It was founded in 1923 to organize and fund the fight against business development in the area, and continued through the '30s and beyond to oppose large homes being turned into boarding houses, offices, nursing homes and apartments. Throughout its history, it has opposed much that ultimately made Jane Jacobs and much of the rest of the city such fans of the neighbourhood. One of its latest causes was to oppose two long-time homeowners turning their mock-Tudor house into a modern-looking one. They've done benevolent things as well –they conduct walks and plant flowers in local gardens[1] – but they are, like most such organizations, an essentially conservative force.

Associations like this abound across the city and, at their very core, they are, like those concerned citizens of the Kingsway, chiefly concerned with preservation rather than evolution. They can be powerful organizations, however, and they could probably achieve quite a bit more than they already do if they brainstormed as much as they raged. As it stands, their members often behave in ways that are self-serving and small-minded.

Though he's neither of those things, John Sewell, once mayor of the city and forever the guy who stopped the Spadina Expressway, which would have gutted the Annex by running a six-lane freeway right through the middle of it, figures it's just common sense why so much community activism is about saying no. Doing the opposite mostly means coming up with your own ideas, and though that's by definition more difficult than saying no to someone else's, that's not the main obstacle.

'It's very, very difficult to put things on the public agenda,' Sewell tells me in his upper room in the George Brown House at the corner of Beverley and Baldwin that he's used as an office for more than a decade. *Globe* writer Ian Brown's down the hall; indie magazine *Broken Pencil*'s in there somewhere as well. Sewell

1 They had a big hand in the design of the recent refurbishment of Gwendolyn MacEwen Park on Walmer Road, for instance, and have performed horticultural labours in Sibelius Park as well. But with these and other good works, the ARA and other ratepayers' groups exhibit their fundamental tendency of wanting to keep their neighbourhoods nice, just like they are, rather than taking chances on evolution or expansion.

is talking about that complex combination of strategy and perseverance that enables someone, or a group of someones, to get enough people to pay attention to something that it gets discussed and ultimately acted upon. 'The only way [an idea] can get on the public agenda is by reacting to something that's already there.'

John Sewell

He's a big proponent of opponents, though.

'When we talked about protecting neighbourhoods with urban renewal,' he says, taking a page from his own past, 'we were saying you should not be tearing things down; instead, you should be strengthening this neighbourhood.

His example is his first bit of public activism: saying no to the City's plans to bulldoze and rebuild a little slice of residential neighbourhood between the part of Cabbagetown that had been turned into Regent Park and St. James Town and the part of Corktown that had been made into Moss Park. Trefann Court, it was called. 'That's exactly what happened when we won,' he says of his 1966 fight with alderwoman and other future mayor June Rowlands. 'We got to create a new plan for the area by building a lot more affordable housing.'

They did a lot more than that. The big no at Trefann Court effectively marked the end of the sort of urban renewal that destroyed in order to rebuild and that fell into such disrepute in the decades that followed and is now being undone wherever possible. 'You can say that's a no thing,' Sewell says, 'but on the other hand, we're talking about a different vision of the city.'

Misha Glouberman is a fun guy who has spent a lot of his time trying to ensure his own neighbourhood does not fall victim to hoards of fun-seekers who would, if they were allowed, turn their favourite parts of the city into funlands, suitable for parties, bars and hip late-night joints, but ignoring the basic needs of the local residents who often were the ones who made these neighbourhoods so cool and attractive in the first place. People like Glouberman, for instance, a creative cultural urban activist – one of the forces behind the hipster lecture series Trampoline Hall and the principal of the Misha Glouberman School of Learning where he teaches classes in 'unuseful things' – who's now spent a good deal of time opposing the clubification of his West Queen West neighbourhood (around Beaconsfield, in Drake territory). He agrees heartily, putting it slightly more poetically. 'You can control things, like waters flowing,' he says, 'but you can only control them by building dams. You don't bring your own water.'

So no is not always bad, or even necessarily negative. But it is always reactive, and it's often reactionary.

Is there a way, one that might have a chance of actually getting something done, changing something, of being proactive in the city?

Even though Sewell warns against it, describing it as either difficult or impossible, he does offer advice on what he considers the essential first steps.

'You've got to work with other people, that's the first thing: you can't do things alone,' he says. 'The question is how do you get linked into a group that will give you some knowledge of what the issues are and some ability to make some political ground that you can work from. I think people have to get involved with whatever they want; it might be the community centre near their place of work that's involved with an issue. I happen to be interested in education, so I'll go work with Pathways to Education.

There's fertile ground wherever you want to make it, as long as you aren't trying to invent things from scratch.'

But obviously someone's going to have to start things from scratch in order for people like Sewell to join. Sewell just suggests – advice born from years of trial and error – that it's less painful to let someone else do the heavy lifting.

I press him a little about alternatives to no. But a lifetime of disappointments and defeats punctuated by the occasional remarkable victory born of a no has had its effect. He's not to be drawn out. So I badger him.

'Talk to Jutta,' he says.

Jutta is Jutta Mason, demiurge of Dufferin Grove Park.

I tell her Sewell sent me to learn how to say yes, how to get things done without using collective anger at someone else's stupidity as your starting block.

'I certainly get mad,' she says. 'But when you put it like that ...' She pauses and makes some reflecting sounds. 'My own background is that my family came from Germany. I was a kid, but it was pretty soon after the Second World War. To be German, and to understand what happened in Germany, it's so dreadful, in my view.

'It made it really, really urgent to figure out how strangers could come to know each other to find out how some sort of loyalty could spring up. Germans watched their neighbours being gassed and dragged off and then took over their houses.

'It would make sense, then, if you want to find a way that strangers can possibly, if not become friends then at least recognize each other in some way, and perhaps even come to admire each other, then the project gets fairly narrow. Where are you likely to encounter and see admirable things about your neighbours? It's less likely in a mall; churches are more interesting, as are schools, but they have a pretty strong institutional mandate and I have a pretty anti-institutional mandate.'

Her answer, of course, was the neighbourhood park.

She both followed Sewell's formula and went beyond it. She started by volunteering with the local kids' hockey program and from there expanded outward, but not by much, maintaining that narrow focus she believes is key.

'I hate rallying people around,' she says. 'If people are rallying, I want to go home. It's exhilarating for about ten minutes, but after that, it gets so tedious.'

She prefers doing things small and, whenever possible, surreptitiously.

'If you can figure out a way to get more benches in a park by just befriending someone who knows where there's a room where benches are stored,' she says, 'you get this secret satisfaction, or just even the next morning seeing the groupings and realizing there must have been conversations, that people moved the benches closer. It allows you to take this hidden pleasure in normal, everyday, non-dramatic goings-on between people.'

Her benches also highlight an important aspect of the way she's able to make things work. It's difficult to keep up something like community activism, and if you have to do everything yourself – or yourselves – it can become overwhelming, and when people are overwhelmed, they tend to retreat into their own lives. So Mason recommends using the people whose jobs it is to be doing the sorts of things you want done.

When we talked in early April, mayoral hopeful George Smitherman had just issued a press release about his idea to pick fifteen signature parks across the city and endow them with advisory councils, and a citywide 'adopt a park' program that would make decisions about the parks and pitch in to improve them. Anyone else might have thought it was a great idea: get people involved in their parks and they take ownership of them, coming together to improve the city's public spaces. Perfect, like a natural extension of former mayor Miller's Community Cleanup

Day. As the press release put it, 'public participation in parks management would seem like common sense to most people.'

Not to Mason.

'To my mind, it's a pretty good recipe for troubles,' she says, warning that it's very easy for volunteers who don't know how things work, what's possible and what's not, to get bogged down. 'It also sidelines the tax-paid-for workers.'

This is something I, for one, would never have thought of in these terms, which is maybe an example of why some people can make something out of nothing, while most of us can just try our best to make nothing out of somethings we don't like.

'Instead of challenging the workers to do their jobs over the years,' Mason says of the people who have worked on Dufferin Grove Park with her, 'we've fought to have workers that are amazing, and they're all paid by the City. So there's not a whole lot of times when people do come together to do their own park work. Because they actually go to the park to befriend one another, they don't come to the park to mow the lawn.'

There are two organizations apparently related to the work going on with Dufferin Grove Park, though with that strong anti-institutional mandate of hers, Mason is quick to point out that Friends of Dufferin Grove Park, which the newspapers have implied is the group behind the pizza ovens, the Friday-night dinners, the farmers' markets and clothing swaps, is just the name of a website. And the Centre for Local Research into Public Space, the body behind the website, of which Mason is the putative administrator, is actually a collection of contacts: no staff, no office, no phone number. Easy. With little infrastructure, there's less to maintain, less to administer, less to fight over and less to fall apart. Dufferin Grove Park as it is today seems to exist purely as the continually renewed product of affirmative communal will focused through the lens of one postwar German.

If you were the sort to read the Toronto sections of the newspapers and watch the local news bits online and on TV, you would be forgiven for thinking, through much of this past decade, that Mason was an anomaly, an *Übermensch* sent from the Fatherland to teach us the value of communal activity. But you'd be wrong, as Mason is the first to point out. Though opposition, whether pettifogging or ultimately creative, remains the norm, there are others who through either lucky circumstance or iron will start things from scratch.

Mason's own personal hero in this regard is Amy Sutherland, a thirty-year-old mother of three and former Grade 3 teacher who grew up and lives among the towers of Thorncliffe Park. 'Amy's sort of a young genius,' Mason says, pointing me in her direction.

When Sutherland found herself off work after the birth of her first child four years ago, she took to spending time in R. V. Burgess Park, which Mason describes as 'a crummy little park,' and the only park in a neighbourhood with a 1,800-child elementary school and 25 per cent of its population under the age of four. She got to know some other mothers of similarly aged kids, and talk eventually turned to how crummy this little park really was. It was also a crossroads; most residents had to walk across it to get wherever they were going, and so it was mostly muddy, and filled with trash, which was cleaned by the City once a week – not nearly enough. So the mothers, overwhelmingly recent immigrants from the Middle East and Southeast Asia, organized cleanup crews.

'We only had a few of them,' says Sutherland, speaking of the cleanup days, 'and they weren't super-well-attended.'

But the desire for collective action was sparked nonetheless, and the women started having meetings with their city councillor.

'We didn't expect anything,' she says. 'We didn't even expect them to return our phone calls.' So when not only were their

Amy Sutherland at R. V. Burgess Park

phone calls returned, but meetings were scheduled, they were chuffed. 'We saw that the City, well, they didn't do a lot, but they did a few things.' And after meetings with the mothers, they did a few more things, like put in more garbage cans, and a little anti-mud landscaping in the park. 'It was a long process, but seeing the progress being made encouraged us to keep going.'

The next thing the group did was hire performers to entertain the children in the park on Friday nights during the spring and summer. 'I think people have a lot of excitement,' Sutherland says, 'kids as well. They also look forward to what's going to happen in the park – they don't necessarily have the opportunity to travel a lot or attend many things.' By travel, she means on the TTC.

The women, by now known as the Thorncliffe Park Women's Committee ('I love that name,' Mason tells me, 'it's so old-fashioned'), decided to build on the park-based activities. In February, they had a winter carnival with warm drinks, marsh-mallow roasting and ice-cube sculptures.

Next, they set their eyes on a bazaar where women could set up tables and sell food and handicrafts and clothes. As it turned out, their plans coincided with the municipal strike, and so the bylaw officers who might otherwise have had an issue with some of what they were doing were not a problem. So for two Fridays in July, the community got together for an overwhelmingly popular bazaar. This led to a festival for Pakistan's Independence Day and a second winter carnival. When I spoke to Sutherland, the Women's Committee were planning another set of bazaars, though she figured with permits now a necessity, there were certain things, like selling clothes women bring back from their trips to their countries of origin, that would have to be dropped.

In addition to all these events, the Thorncliffe Park Women's Committee has also succeeded in creating a place for women with no natural entrée into Canadian society.

'One of the most exciting stories,' Sutherland tells me, 'is a lady who is on our committee, she actually joined our committee on her second day in Canada. She had moved here to Thorncliffe, she was walking through the park, saw us having our meeting and came and joined us. Through working with our group, she's gained a real insight into community, and she's gone on to do a one-year diploma in community development and now is really active and encourages other women to get involved.'

Sutherland tells me about another woman who used to work with the World Health Organization in Bangladesh. She has small children, and has yet to be credentialed here. But now, according to Sutherland, she's doing the same work as she was doing back in Bangladesh, educating the community through projects of the Women's Committee about environmental health issues.

In March 2010, the Women's Committee got a $150,000 Trillium Foundation grant to continue their work. Sutherland expects to hire at least one staff member and generally continue in their narrow but spiritedly upward spiral.

The issue here seems to be one of imaginative effort. You could say that Sutherland et al. said no to garbage in the park, but they said it in a positive way. They didn't just demand the garbage be tidied, or put up signs threatening litterers with fines and making sure they were enforced. They made the park more central to their community, a place where things happened and people were happy. The cleanup became a minor no among a chorus of much more interesting yeses.

Though Toronto is hardly alone in its devotion to no-based activism, there are places where Mason and Sutherland would be more the rule than the exception. Portland, Oregon, for instance, is a city known for the essential yesness of its civic activism.

According to Mayor Sam Adams, everything from the bike lanes to the 7,000-seat Portland Center for the Performing Arts has its origins in citizen initiatives.

'I guess I've never really thought about it,' Adams says, 'but Portland has much more prospective change organizations than ones that stop things from happening.'

This may be partly due to the Office of Neighbourhood Involvement, which has an annual budget of $2.5 million to offer staff and organizational assistance to 95 neighbourhood associations, helping them do things like run meetings and draw up proposed bylaws for the City to consider.

There also seems to be a generally permissive attitude towards proactive ideas in what Adams calls a 'do-it-yourself and do-it-yourself-together kind of culture,' even when they might infringe on bylaws and ordinances. 'There's a universal agreement that if it's a good thing,' Adams says, 'I just let it go.'

This yesness may run even more deeply. Adams figures it may have its origins in the days when the Hudson's Bay Company ran the town. Back then, in the late 18th and early 19th century, Americans lived side by side with the British subjects who ran and worked for the company's operations.

'There was an understanding,' he says, 'that U.S. citizens followed American law, and British subjects followed British law, even if they lived next door to each other. I'm convinced that's the root of this sort of open thing we have going in Portland.'

He may have a point. Maybe our no-ness is a result of a historically closed society, run by Protestants during our own formative years, whose fun-free claws are still felt all over our liquor laws. Or maybe it's just because we're big and complicated and Portland's little and simple.

But Portland bears some looking at. The big project there at the moment is Gateway Green, a strip of land owned by the state that a collection of individuals decided might make a nice park. After five years of organizing, not against an encroaching developer – there is none – but towards a nice new park, the first draft of an agreement came through the day before I talked to Linda Robinson, one of the prime movers behind the project.

'We have a long history of public involvement here,' she says. And they've had their share of no's, including a very Spadina Expressway–esque Mount Hood Freeway opposition, which succeeded in stopping the neighbourhood-razing road in 1974. According to Robinson, though, that was an anomaly. For the most part, community activism in Portland takes the form of creating things out of nothing. Even from that big freeway no, those opposed to it managed to redirect the money earmarked for the freeway towards a new light rail system. The two-acre Senn's Dairy Park, on an old residential brownfield, is another addition to the city that came entirely from neighbours who thought a neighbourhood called Parkrose ought to have at least one park in it. Robinson lists off three more such projects, some bigger, some smaller, in the fifteen minutes we speak in September. Her advice to aspirational yea-sayers?

'You've got to have patience, and you've got to have persistence,' she says. 'You can't go beating people over the head and threatening them, but at the same time, you can't let them forget about it. We spent a lot of time doing strong background work before we went public with Gateway Green, meeting with decision-makers, just to gauge how much support there might be for it.' They then took the support they found to the state. 'They had been approached by various groups, bicycle groups for instance, in the past and had always said no, and they told us that we'd done enough background work that we might actually be able to pull it off. We got a tentative yes where others had got a no because we had done the work.'

It was only after they got that tentative yes that they called their first public meeting; the project already had some momentum behind it, which attracted volunteers eager to participate in something that had a real possibility of success.

See? Easy.

There are large organizations, like the United Way, that work from the same basic principles as Mason, Sutherland and Robinson. But then, you'd expect that from a charity. What came as more of a surprise to me, when I started to think about who did what around the city and how, was that there was a movement born in Bloor West Village in 1970 that evolved like a mirror image of the ratepayers' movement; on the surface, I would have expected it to be the more conservative of the two but it is, in fact, all about proactive and often progressive action on a neighbourhood level. John Sewell doesn't think much of them, and professes not to be able to tell whether one is active in any given neighbourhood or not, but I suspect that might be his well-earned poopiness talking . Because as far as I can tell, the city's Business Improvement Areas are a perfect model for the sort of front-line activism we're talking about here.

There are any number of reasons people might dislike BIAS. They're mostly against bike lanes, for instance, saying street parking is too valuable to local business. And they're businesses, which many of the more traditional sort of urban activists are often sceptical of. But at their root, they're the same as Dufferin Grove and Thorncliffe parks: neighbourhood people getting together to see what they can do to improve their collective lot. As the Toronto Association of Business Improvement Areas, the organization of these seventy-one BIAS, tells its own story on its website (toronto-bia.com), the first BIA got its start in Bloor West Village when jewellery store owner Neil McLellan and lawyer Bill Whiteacre started talking in a local hangout, the Petit Paris bakery, about what to do in the face of suburban flight. 'The Bloor subway line had just been completed,' as a *Toronto Star* story by Jennifer Yang describes it, 'and every time the train rumbled underfoot, it was a painful reminder of shoppers who were no longer viewing their storefronts on the streetcar.' The first thing the business folks did, after they decided to get together, was put up strings of lights in the trees and install flower planters on the sidewalks. A small thing, like Sutherland's cleanup crews, but it turned out to be enough to give the neighbourhood some sense of cohesion. But at least as important, the positive reaction to it threw off a spark among the organizers to do more.

Since then, those lights in Yorkville, the new lamp posts in Bloordale, the solar-panel-powered LED lights in Bloor West Village, Bloor's Ukrainian street festival and the Taste of the Danforth have all sprung out of BIA efforts, using funds the businesses levy against themselves for the purpose. Can you imagine a ratepayers' group voting to pay higher rates?

Take the Albion Islington Square BIA that covers the part of northern Etobicoke that used to be called Thistletown. It's developed a streetscape plan that involves building better pedestrian crossings, public boulevard art and new street furniture. Or Bloor-Yorkville, which invested $20 million of its own money – its members' money – to make a stretch of Bloor between Avenue and Church prettier (with the hope, of course, of attracting customers). The very fact that there's an association of these associations highlights the essentially collaborative nature of the movement. Instead of setting themselves up in opposition to perceived stupidity from the City, or developers, or fence-building residents, they meet to discuss what might be done, not what shouldn't, and through TABIA, they share particulars of what's worked and what hasn't, and how to get things done.

There are lessons to be learned here, many I'm sure addressed by the Maytree Foundation's new DiverseCity Fellow program, set up in 2009 to breed community leaders, but there's no real point in enumerating them here. Neither Mason, nor Sutherland, nor McLellan and Whiteacre had any particular experience in community organizing. None of them seem to have been interested in changing the city, though they all have. The important common denominator is that they came up with ideas and made them real, and in doing so, showed that though saying no can be effective, and is often easier, saying yes can work too. And it's way less bitchy.

Get involved

theara.org
dufferinpark.ca
toronto-bia.com

pathwaystoeducation.ca
tpwomenscomm.ca
maytree.com

Bert Archer came to Toronto for the first time for university and stayed. He's liked it more and more every year till this one, when he's decided to withhold judgment. He's been an editor or columnist at the *Star*, *NOW*, *Eye*, the *Globe*, *Xtra* and *Fab* over the years and has written about various aspects of this highly functional city, including the food it doesn't eat and the water it doesn't drink, for previous Coach House books.

Edward Keenan
Ranked thoughts on voting reform

[1] By the time this book is published, Rob Ford will have been elected mayor of Toronto. Or George Smitherman will have been elected instead. Or perhaps Joe Pantalone. It is theoretically possible that someone else will have won, though that seems less and less likely to me as I type this, a few weeks before the 2010 election. Still, I am no psychic. Though you already know, as you read this, who won the election for mayor, I cannot pretend to be sure. But I can be almost sure that, no matter which white guy becomes His Worship on October 25, 2010, he will probably have done so against the expressed wishes of a majority of voters. In a field with three front-running candidates and thirty-seven other names on the ballot, it seems likely that less than 40 per cent of the vote will be enough to carry the day. Anyone who breaks that 40 per cent barrier will have won a stunning victory.

[2] Of course, I mean 40 per cent of those who actually vote. If you take a minute to look up the turnout from the 2010 election on the City's website, I'm fairly certain you'll see that fewer than half of those eligible to vote bothered to do so. If 40 per cent of eligible voters did so in 2010, it will be the first time in a decade that such a high proportion of Torontonians has cast a ballot. At the risk of seeming repetitive, let me phrase this a different way: it is almost a certainty that 60 per cent or more of voters will have stayed home, as they have done in every municipal election in megacity history. In other words, a super-majority of voters does not vote at all. By the standards of many organizations, our elections don't even reach quorum.

[3] Doing the math then, it seems likely that, assuming we reach the towering height of 40 per cent voter turnout, and the winning candidate achieves the remarkable feat of getting 40 per cent of the votes, the winner will represent the expressed choice of 16 per cent of eligible voters. I would not be surprised if the number is actually significantly lower. If it's a point or two higher, you can mention it to me at a party sometime and we'll laugh at my foolishness. The point is that it seems not only possible but very, very likely that the mayor will be elected by fewer than one-sixth of the voters. Does that seem democratic?

[4] I think the question is legitimate, and the conclusions are not foregone, for many reasons. For a start: unlike many of the people obsessed with voter turnout, I believe strongly in the right not to vote. If I am totally ignorant of the issues and the candidates, why should I subject the rest of the population to my randomly selected choices? If I would be equally happy, or equally unhappy, with whatever selection is made, why should I bother to go out of my way to rob people who feel strongly about their choice? In fact, if I don't know and don't care about something, wouldn't it actually be poor citizenship to vote, to take something as serious and important as the election and warp it with my ignorance?

[5] Apathy. Are we talking about apathy? Perhaps a person who doesn't know or doesn't care about the issues in the election – who is not engaged in the process, as they say in the artsy lefty political circles I travel in – perhaps that person is apathetic. People would say that emotion, or lack of it, is a symptom of a politics that is deeply flawed, a democracy that is off-track. They may be right. Or often right. Yet I'm also, unpopularly, a defender of political apathy, or at least of the right to be apathetic: people have the luxury of not caring about politics only in places where they are largely content with the government they get. Sure, we might all complain about garbage pickup and wait times for subways and potholes and traffic and whether the mayor understands regular folks like us. We complain. But really: the garbage gets picked up, transit takes us where we're going, the roads are still navigable. If you look at places where the stakes in the election are literally life-and-death for a substantial portion of the population – Iran, Afghanistan, India, where people sometimes brave violence while they line up for hours to vote. In the separation referendum in Quebec in 1995, 94 per cent of voters turned out. When people believe there is something really existentially important at stake, they do not feel apathetic about it, and they do not stay home from the polls. I mention this mostly to keep us grounded about what we're talking about: when we say voters are alienated from the process, we mean it in the sense that teenagers mean it when they say they are alienated by Shakespeare: there aren't enough flashing lights and high kicks to command constant attention, and deciphering what it all means doesn't seem to be rewarding enough to justify the effort. That's a problem for those who think what government is doing is important and worthy of attention, certainly, but it's also a sign that the current process is producing enough satisfaction that constituents can find it boring.

[6] That doesn't mean politics *should* be boring. Fresh ideas, vision, solving real problems, building an excellent city – these things ought to be interesting, and it's a crime that we hear so little of these things during municipal election campaigns. But that's a substance problem, not a function of the system. Inspiration and excitement will lead to higher voter turnout (and do). But forcing a higher turnout in and of itself will not make politics more inspiring or exciting. So if you're expecting me to work my way around to laws that require voting, such as they have in Australia, you have come to the wrong place.

[7] I went off on that windy tangent because if we're going to talk about the generally sleep-inducing topic of electoral reform –

and lucky you! I'm talking about it! – we should be clear that we're talking about questions of fairness, not of imagining the world as we'd like it to be. (Is that an ironic thing to say in a book in a series entitled *uTOpia*, dedicated at least somewhat to utopian thinking? I leave that to you to determine.) You, a reader of a book on how to change the world through citizen engagement, and I, a contributor to such a book, wish that everyone cared as much as we do, read as much as we do, went to as many meetings as we do, participated in the process as much as we do. It would be nice if everyone were more like us, wouldn't it? But the nature of our diverse democracy is that we are not all alike, and we all get to choose how we participate or don't, without undue meddling from our neighbours. What we are all entitled to, above all else, is fairness. And while low voter turnout may be troubling, it is not evidence of unfairness.

[8] Which brings us back to point [1]. How is it fair that a candidate can win while a majority of voters voted for someone else? To those of us in Canada (and to those in places like the U.K. and the U.S., which have similar electoral systems), this seems like a weird question. Fair? What could be more fair? The guy with the most votes wins, right? And in a two-person race, or a two-party race, that is pretty much fair. The winner, in that circumstance, has a majority of the votes, by definition. But when you add more candidates, it is harder to discern the will of the majority. What if, for example, there are five candidates, all of roughly equal competence, and four of them are reasonably similar in ideology while one is of diametrically opposed opinion. The four will likely split the votes of those who agree with them, while the one gets all the other votes. Even if the four get 70 per cent of the vote between them, the one ideological loner will stand a good chance of winning. Any of the four could have beaten the loner one-on-one. How is that fair? It's not,

really. And it certainly takes a lot of logical twisting to make it look like democracy.

[9] The existence of this problem leads to something called 'strategic voting,' which everyone pretty much hates and which never really seems to work, given that everyone who has a strong opinion thinks their preferred candidate should benefit from the strategy and given that we have secret ballots, which means no one can really tell what vote would make the most strategic sense. And as functioning democracy goes, this tactic sucks, since the point of strategic balloting is to vote for someone other than the candidate you hope will win, which is not really how the process is designed to work. The word 'perversion' springs to mind. So how about we just avoid saying much more about strategic voting than that.

[10] This situation, outlined in **[8]**, is why many countries have runoff elections. In runoff elections, after the votes are cast, the candidate or candidates who get the least votes are removed from the ballot, and everyone votes again for one of the remaining candidates. This process repeats until someone gets a majority of the votes.

[11] It is worth noting that all the political parties in Canada use runoff balloting in their leadership elections, presumably because they think having a leader who wasn't supported by a majority of the party would be disastrous.

[12] Also, the Academy Awards recently instituted a form of runoff balloting in the Best Picture category because they wanted to better reflect the will of the Academy. They switched from the system we use in our mayoral elections because it seemed insufficiently democratic for such an important event. Really.

[13] The form of voting they use for the Academy Awards is called 'instant runoff,' in which voters rank the candidates on their ballot rather than simply voting for their favourite. When the votes come in, the tabulators take everyone's first choice and add up the numbers. Then they drop the lowest vote-getter from the list and take the second choice of everyone who voted for it and add those numbers to the initial totals. They then drop the new last-place picture from the list and add the second-place votes of those voters to the others – if any of these votes were ones added as second-place votes after the first loser dropped off, their third-place votes are now added. This continues until one movie gets a majority of the votes.

[14] Did that description confuse you? It might, although it is actually fairly simple if you see a demonstration. The difficulty of explaining this system (versus 'the guy with the most votes wins') is actually its biggest drawback.

[14.1] One other possible drawback, discussed in a 2010 *New Yorker* article by Hendrik Hertzberg, is that the supporters of the very least popular candidates are the first to get their second choices – and possibly their third and fourth choices – recounted. Why this matters is that in some mathematically possible situations involving interesting voting triangles, the second choices of fascists and communists and the other radicals whose picks finish last could push a candidate over 50 per cent when it is possible that the reapportioning of the votes of a more popular candidate would have led to a different result. This is riveting reading, though it is not less fair, and is almost certain to occur less often than what occurs now very frequently at the Council level and probably occurred in 2010 at the mayoral level, which is that a candidate won with a minority of the vote and a small plurality.

[15] Facing up to the tough challenge of discussing this and other electoral reforms in Toronto is a group called Better Ballots, led in part by Dave Meslin, who is also one of the editors of this book. Better Ballots has been studying and leading discussions about alternative voting methods that might be more fair – and, as they say, lead to a more diverse council that is more reflective of the city's population and more responsive to it. In a series of town hall meetings held in April 2010, Better Ballots asked people to vote on a number of possible changes to our electoral system. Ranked ballots – instant runoff – won the most support among the possible voting systems discussed.

[16] If instant runoff balloting were implemented in Toronto, as it has been in San Francisco and Minneapolis, it might have its most dramatic effect on the makeup of Council. Unseating an incumbent in Council is nearly impossible. Many members of Council hold their jobs for twenty years or more, cemented in place by the power of their names and the general disinterest of the population (see **[1]**, **[2]** and **[3]**). In the 2006 election, for example, only one incumbent was beaten, and his opponent was a former Member of Provincial Parliament. In 2003, four candidates, including Karen Stintz, defeated incumbents. In 1997, the amalgamation election, Sandra Bussin was the only winning candidate who was not already a sitting councillor. In many cases, incumbents win not just because of the advantages of being the person already doing the job and serving the constituents, but because those who oppose them line up behind multiple candidates. In the past, long-serving Council members like Howard Moscoe, Bill Saundercook and Case Ootes have been able to win – sometimes in successive elections – with well under a majority of the votes. In open seats, the situation becomes even less certain: Gord Perks won in Ward 14 in 2006 with just over 30 per cent of the vote. John Parker won that same year in Ward 26 with only 20 per cent.

[17] It may surprise you at this stage in the essay to learn that I originally intended to write about Karen Stintz's success in beating long-serving incumbent Anne Johnston in 2003. What impressed me about Stintz was that she was just about the only giant-slayer I could find who had never held elected office, never been someone's executive assistant and was not a relative of a popular politician. In most of the few-and-far-between cases where an incumbent is defeated, you dig and find that the person who won had a built-in political machine already in place, that they were hand-picked to run, that they were on something like equal footing from the start. Stintz, by contrast, was a nobody – a provincial civil servant who answered a 'Councillor Wanted' ad from an angry ratepayers' group. I went to speak to her because I thought her campaign might provide a blueprint for grassroots action. She told me how she broke all the rules: got into the campaign in September; lost money on her first fundraiser, then raised only $17,000 in total; ran the whole operation from her living room rather than getting an office. As she explained, her success came from a few factors: 1] The demographics of the ward had changed and, as a young professional, she looked more like the average voter than Johnston did. 2] She had compelling, advertising-agency-quality literature with professional language and her own signature on it. 3] She got some media attention out of the story of the ratepayers' ad. 4] She was allied with John Tory in a ward where he was popular. 5] She doesn't think Johnston ever took her seriously as a challenger. And that's it.

[18] The reason this essay is not all about Karen Stintz is that in speaking to her, I realized that what makes her interesting is the singularity of her victory. She's not an example of how one can beat an incumbent – there are no bits of political wizardry behind the curtain. In the same way that Barack Obama's biography does not present a roadmap for how young black men from broken homes can typically go about succeeding, Stintz's victory, by virtue of being the only one of its kind anyone can remember, points simply to how infrequently this sort of thing happens, and how high the odds are stacked against it.

[19] That said, I should admit for the sake of being honest about my own perspective that shortly after I spoke to Stintz, I seriously considered running for City Council in the 2010 election, against an incumbent. I received kind support from many people I will not embarrass by naming, and became convinced I could win. Then I decided that at this point in my life, with two small children and still much writing that I want to do, I do not want to get involved in politics. So I did not feel that the need for electoral reform applied to me.

[20] Of course, everyone thinks they could win if they ran, so it is likely, just looking at electoral history and statistics, that I would not have won.

[21] One big obsession of the work of Better Ballots that my parallel-universe victory would not have addressed is the lack of diversity on Council. In a city that has a visible minority population of 47 per cent, we had as of early 2010 only four non-whiteys sitting in City Hall's chamber. And of our forty-four councillors, only ten were women. There are lots of way to explain that – women are, as a group, more risk-averse, recently arrived populations of visible minority citizens tend to be establishing their lives here rather than trying to join the government, etc., etc. – but really, the numbers are kind of shocking and, to many, embarrassing. One possible way to address the problem would be simply to increase the amount of turnover. The make-up of Council hasn't been changing as quickly as the

population has. More turnover on Council might lead to more diverse faces, not just new ones. Maybe.

[22] Another method of ensuring quick turnover would be to implement term limits, as exist in U.S. cities such as New York. Unlike ranked balloting, this idea actually became part of the discussion early on during the 2010 mayoral election when it was brought up by mayoral candidate Rocco Rossi. Just over half of the Better Ballots panellists voted in favour of it, too. However, it was an idea that most politicians oppose and are unlikely to implement because it means, in many cases, firing themselves or limiting their own job security. It also poses the tricky problem of removing from Council all of the people who have been there long enough to know how to navigate the bureaucracy.

[23] Another touchy subject that was very unpopular with the Better Ballots panels is the introduction of political parties at the municipal level. *Toronto Star* columnist Royson James mentioned at a panel discussion in September 2010 that the introduction of political parties would add coherence to the debate at City Hall and during election campaigns, since challengers would have a brand to represent rather than having to build one from scratch, and since Council would have clear lines between government and opposition. He also pointed out that party politics would likely diversify Council in a hurry. At the provincial and federal levels, parties tend to engage in a form of affirmative action to appeal to their own best instincts and to ethnic communities in specific areas. Karen Stintz also mentioned party politics to me as a possible reform, though she was of two minds on the issue, claiming to prefer the collegiality of the independent system. Virtually everyone seems to prefer that collegiality, even though it is seldom seen.

[24] I could go on and on listing possible reforms that are being bandied about: the I Vote Toronto campaign aims to give the vote to non-citizen permanent residents and has drawn the support of former mayor David Miller. Former chief planner Paul Bedford has recommended that the City implement 'neighbourhood advisory councils.' FairVote Canada has proposed a proportional model, using larger multi-member wards. Others have said it is time to have councillors-at-large who would not be beholden to local ward interests and would represent the city more broadly, perhaps by being elected to specific portfolios (Budget Chief, Parks Department Chair, TTC Chair). All of these are worth looking into, even if I do not have the time or space to go into them in detail here.

[25] What the existence of all these proposals from different corners shows is that the desire for reform is great, at least among those already engaged in the system. So much about the current model seems patently unfair, and often undemocratic. And then, at the end of the process, when Council sits down in the chamber, it doesn't even work all that efficiently. Ranked balloting seems like a no-brainer, though I have no idea how it goes from activist proposal to actuality – a campaign led (again) by Dave Meslin called RaBIT that launched immediately before election day gained support from all the leading mayoral candidates, so perhaps that will finally make the issue central. Someone ought to study how they did it at the Academy Awards.

[26] It is worth remembering, however, that technical tweaks can make the system more democratic and fair, and that a more fair and democratic process might make the process more inviting to more people. But after all of that, if we want a more engaged electorate, if we want a more involved citizenry, what we need is something more than process tweaks. We need the content of our politics to change. We need to be discussing – as a city, led by those who assume to be our leaders – what we can build together in the most diverse, most livable city in the world, one that is a financial capital and an innovation hub, one with links to nearly every other country in the world. It's fine that we ask how we can better choose among politicians who want our attention. But what we need, too, are politicians who want to explore what kind of city we can become together. That's not electoral reform, that's political culture reform. As distant as the first seems, is it possible that it can help inspire the latter?

Get involved

betterballots.to

fairvote.ca

RaBIT.ca

ivotetoronto.org

Edward Keenan has lived in Toronto all his life – residing in Riverdale, the Annex, Scarborough, Harbord Village and Bloordale at various times. Today he lives in the Junction with his wife, Rebecca, and their children, Colum and Irene. He works as a senior editor at *Eye Weekly* and a contributing editor of *Spacing*, and writers regularly about politics, books, sexuality, business and other topics that strike his fancy.

Hamutal Dotan

We built this city?
Community engagement in planning, zoning and
urban development

The first thing Abdirizack Hersi does is offer to make me a mug
of traditional Somali tea. Brewed with cardamom and cloves, it's
sweet and comforting, with warm, spicy undertones. He keeps
a stash of it in the kitchen of the community meeting centre he
frequents, where he can often be found discussing housing,
poverty and other issues of local concern. Hersi was, once upon
a time, an entomologist in Somalia; today he is a tenant representative working to engage local residents – his friends and
neighbours – in the revitalization of the Lawrence Heights
neighbourhood of Toronto.

Lawrence Heights is a sprawling, windy-road enclave near
the geographic centre of town, one hundred acres' worth of low-
rises and single-family homes, almost all of which are public
housing. Though it lies well within the city's limits, Lawrence
Heights has a distinctly suburban feel: wide streets, quiet traffic
and vast tracts of lawn keep the downtown hustle firmly at bay.
It's one of Toronto's thirteen designated 'priority neighbourhoods,' areas that have been selected for particular attention and
investment by the City.

The neighbourhood's suburban qualities are not incidental:
Lawrence Heights was intended to be this way. Built in the
mid-to-late 1950s, it was a grand experiment in social housing
that reflected Modernist ideals of urban planning. Specifically,
it was received wisdom at the time that residences should be
kept separate from the noisy, dirty, gritty working world, that
density was unhealthy and that the ideal home was bordered by
a significant swath of flat green yard.

Abdirizack Hersi

By just about every measure, the experiment has been a profound failure.

Streets are desolate and empty, and grassy hillsides are conspicuously devoid of playing children or gossiping teens – there are simply too few people to enliven these carefully planned green spaces. Sequestering residential development from commercial land uses has meant there's almost nothing by way of local business, either: there are no coffee shops or corner grocers or bank branches to draw people to the street. And the neighbourhood's circuitous roads – once thought to be guardians of tranquility – have proved instead a frustrating barrier, cutting residents off from neighbouring communities and the transit system, and generally creating an air of isolation. (Distance from the nearest subways station to the community centre where Hersi keeps his tea, via paved roads: 1.4 kilometres. Distance as the crow flies: approximately 200 metres.)

None of which is to say that Lawrence Heights isn't a vibrant, engaged neighbourhood. It very much is. There are community events and local groups of every kind, there is excited support for high school plays and sports teams and there are many neighbourhood initiatives on the go – some purely recreational, and some more serious, tackling pressing local issues. (Hersi, for instance, is leading the charge against the bedbugs that have started popping up.) But it's all a bit hidden, a bit hard to find. There aren't many engaged and engaging public spaces in Lawrence Heights, few corners at which you can casually bump into your neighbours and no parks with a critical mass of people enjoying them.

All this, combined with rapidly deteriorating buildings and a city-wide mandate to increase density where there is room to do so, led the municipal government to a make a dramatic decision: over the next twenty-five years, Lawrence Heights will be almost entirely levelled and rebuilt. Piece by piece, tract by tract, approximately 1,200 units of public housing will be dismantled and replaced with new facilities. Additional market-price units will also be built, creating a new socio-economic mix in Lawrence Heights. On top of all that, roads will be reconfigured to allow for better access, and some non-residential development will be introduced to the neighbourhood as well. It's the perfect example of what you might call benevolent destruction: well-intentioned, necessary and (if all goes well) ultimately very beneficial – but also requiring that an entire community consent to being ripped up for years.

Securing that consent – engaging with local residents and involving them in the planning of the new Lawrence Heights – is the task of Toronto Community Housing, the largest public-housing provider in Canada. Carmen Smith, formerly a special assistant in the mayor's office, bears the title of Community Revitalization Consultant: her job is to work with other TCH staff and Lawrence Heights residents to create and implement a far-reaching consultation process that ensures the community has input into the redevelopment at every stage and step. If the process goes well, at the end of the revitalization current Lawrence Heights tenants will feel as much a part of their community as they do now, and will have a newly built neighbourhood that still feels like *their* neighbourhood. 'We did not want it to be a process [by which] we would come in and decide, "Here's what the community's going to look like" – that's not going to work,' says Smith. 'You're talking about people's homes, their social network, their community.'

Smith and her team have facilitated large forums, small community discussions and design charrettes; put out newsletters; and canvassed local residents for opinions on matters large and small. But perhaps the most striking thing about this engagement process is that TCH decided to recruit some of those local residents, like Hersi, to help facilitate much of this consultation. About twenty community animators were hired, trained and have been working for the past two years: running focus groups, putting together a community tour and doing outreach via their existing networks in Lawrence Heights. The community animators have also been instrumental in helping to compose and conduct surveys on everything from preferred recreational facilities to individual unit design – about five hundred respondents are sought for each topic or question.

It's slow, painstaking work, bringing hundreds or perhaps thousands of people into this conversation. Many residents were resistant to the idea of revitalization – fearful of losing their homes, of getting pushed out of their communities entirely, of social as well as physical dislocation – and many have yet to be convinced.

'First of all, when we heard "revitalization," we said, "Wow, what's going on with this?"' recalls Hersi. 'Everyone was furious – myself included.' Smith and her colleagues worked within the community to explain the rationale behind the plans, and provided reassurance that the process would be carefully managed to keep disruptions to a minimum. (For instance, during construction, residents will be relocated to other units within the neighbourhood rather than moved to social housing facilities in other parts of the city.)

Bit by bit, some residents began to accept the changes that were coming, and to involve themselves in shaping the course of those changes. It's by no means a universal shift: many Lawrence Heights locals are still deeply sceptical, and many remain unconvinced that wholesale redevelopment is needed. But it is, at the very least, a good start, a robust long-term engagement that is gradually bringing more residents into the planning process rather than simply informing them of its results.

Lawrence Heights represents one particular kind of development in Toronto: that built under the leadership of the municipality itself. Publicly run projects are often sweeping: huge undertakings that affect unusually large areas and, by extension, unusually large numbers of people. They are headline-grabbers, and they often have profound and visible impacts on the texture of the city as a whole.

But they are not the most common kind of development. Those come out of the private sector.

To build on or significantly alter a site in Toronto, a developer needs to file an application with the City, which includes technical plans for the site, an explanation of the planning rationale for the development, and assorted studies and reports. (These depend on the kind of development in question, and cover everything from parking availability to impacts on community services to conservation strategies on designated heritage properties.) A developer may choose to consult with the local community prior to filing an application, but is not required to do so. After it is submitted, the City evaluates the application to determine its conformity with established planning priorities and regulations.

The laws, bylaws and official documents that set out Toronto's planning policies are many and extremely complex. The entire system is governed by the provincial Planning Act, which lays out the development approval process, including some baseline public consultation requirements. (More on these shortly.) Ontario also issues policy statements, which deal with matters of general public interest such as environmental impacts, and with which all municipal plans must conform. Toronto's municipal government, in turn, has an Official Plan, which it developed in the three years after amalgamation. The Official Plan is a long-term strategic document that describes overall planning priorities and outlines an approach to managing growth in and intensification of the city's built form. More specific planning priorities are detailed in secondary and precinct plans, which are drawn up (at least in theory) for each part of the city. Finally, zoning bylaws set out specific rules for every part of the city, including technical details such as acceptable land uses (residential, commercial, industrial, etc.), allowable building heights and maximum densities.

To receive approval, a developer's application must either be interpreted by the City as conforming with its existing planning policies, or the City must be convinced to amend its Official Plan and zoning bylaws to accommodate the proposed development. When a developer applies for an amendment to existing plans – that is, whenever a proposed development falls outside what the City considers standard in a given area – the City usually organizes a community consultation meeting to solicit feedback on the proposal. (It is not, however, required to do so by law.) This community consultation, along with technical feedback from City staff, is received by the developer, which then submits a revised application to the City. City staff review the final application and make a recommendation to approve or reject it.

At that point, the City is required to hold a 'public meeting' to consider the application. This is a meeting of one of City Council's committees (e.g., the Scarborough Community Council, which overseas matters in that part of the city) at which members of the public can give deputations. Unfortunately – and despite the name – these meetings often don't feel like genuine exercises in public consultation. Take one recent and prominent example: 204 Beech Street. The Teehan family purchased this property in January 2010 with the intention of tearing down the house and building a new, wheelchair-accessible home on the site designed to accommodate Melissa Teehan, who is a paraplegic. The house is on an historic street in the east end of Toronto; the Teehans verified that it was not a designated heritage site (and therefore protected from demolition) before purchasing it. Many of their neighbours vigorously objected to the house's destruction, however, and the Teehans' plan to tear it down wound up on the agenda of a community council meeting. Unbeknownst to the Teehans, their local councillor had also taken an interest in their project and raised concerns about it at the meeting – a meeting they say they didn't even know about until after it took place.

Committee meetings are governed by the relevant municipal rules, which limit the form that participation takes: each member of the public can speak only once and is limited to five minutes (after which members of Council can pose questions of the deputant if they wish). There is no free-form dialogue, and while members of the public can use their five minutes to ask questions, there is no requirement that compels the committee to provide answers. The committee takes a vote on the proposal, and its recommendation is then heard at a full meeting of City Council. Council votes on the application; if it is approved, the relevant changes are made to the Official Plan and zoning bylaws, and the development proceeds.

Should an application be rejected, the developer can appeal – not to the City, but to a provincially appointed, quasi-judicial body called the Ontario Municipal Board. The OMB has for many years been widely regarded as being pro-development (though in earlier eras, such as the 1970s, this was much less the case), and municipal decisions are often overturned when developers appeal them. The OMB may decide to allow interested citizens and community groups to testify at an appeal, but it can also refuse them standing on various technical grounds. Most importantly, the OMB is not bound to consider community views in its decisions.

Buried in all this technical detail and amongst all the layers of the approval process is this simple and troubling fact: the sanctioned mechanisms for community engagement in planning and development decisions can generously be described as anaemic. If a private-sector developer wants to build a major project in your community, your only official channels of communication are a City-organized community consultation and a meeting of one of the committees of City Council, both of which take place after a development application has already been filed, at a time when a developer will be extremely disinclined to make any significant changes to its proposal.

As things stand, a developer can draw up detailed plans without community consultation, can file a preliminary application without community consultation, can file a finalized application without accommodating expressed community concerns and can appeal decisions on its application to a body that is not required to consider community views in its verdicts.

One of the most infamous recent cases of development that is proceeding in defiance of clear community wishes involves an area called the West Queen West Triangle. Located southwest of the downtown core and bordered by Queen Street to the north,

Dovercourt Road to the east and the railway corridor to the south and west, the area has until recently been home to many low-income residents, including a significant and vibrant community of artists. Due to increasing gentrification in the neighbourhood (symbolized most potently by the revitalization of the old Drake Hotel, which reopened as a boutique luxury establishment in 2004), developers became increasingly interested in the WQWT. In the spring of 2005 three separate developers filed applications with the City to rezone several parcels of land in the WQWT, with the goal of tearing down existing industrial warehouses (including one – 48 Abell Street – built in 1887 that had been converted to live-work studios for many local artists) and replacing them with condominiums.

City staff found that these applications did not conform to the Official Plan's intentions for the neighbourhood, which called for some increase in density, but also mixed-use, mixed-income development and employment expansion. The proposed condo towers were, in the planning department's opinion, too dense, too high and would put too much pressure on existing urban infrastructure. The applications also lacked important community facilities such as park space for this influx of new residents. In the face of an increasing number of very ambitious development applications, City planners decided they needed to develop a detailed Area Plan for the WQWT before sanctioning any major projects that might fundamentally alter the character of the neighbourhood.

City planners were not the only ones who found the development applications concerning – local residents did as well. In the fall of 2005, many of them banded together and formed a group called Active 18 (the WQWT is located in municipal ward 18) to fight the proposals and pressure the City to create the Area Plan that was lacking, as well as to advocate for increased community engagement in planning processes.

Among Active 18's members were many of the neighbourhood's most engaged residents and business owners, including Jane Farrow (director of Jane's Walk), Margie Zeidler (a heritage-oriented real estate developer) and lawyer Charles Campbell. Active 18 made a point of emphasizing that it was not an anti-development group – this was not a case of NIMBYism. What the group wanted was an engaged, cohesive planning process that would establish a shared community vision that could guide development intelligently.

Meanwhile, the developers filed appeals to have their applications considered by the OMB, which they could do because the City had taken longer than the legally stipulated six months to review their proposals. (It is not uncommon for the City to take that long to process applications; it is much rarer for developers to use that as a reason to appeal.)The appeals were heard in late 2006 and January 2007, and the OMB released its decision: all the developments would be allowed to go forward with only some small alterations.

It was a devastating verdict, and a huge blow to local residents. But it was also very instructive, laying bare many of the flaws and vulnerabilities in Toronto's planning system. In that sense, the saga of the WQWT can provide concerned residents with a blueprint for reform, an outline of the ways in which the current state of affairs needs to change if it is to foster genuine, vital community engagement that has a measurable effect on planning processes and decisions.

In many ways, the WQWT planning process was doomed to fail even before the first developer filed its first application. The ingredients that contributed to that failure were already in place: the absence of an Area Plan, the fact that final decision-making authority rested with OMB and the lack of any consultation with the community prior to the developers drawing up their plans in the first place.

An Area Plan would have equipped City planners with a comprehensive, cohesive, clearly articulated strategic direction for the development of the WQWT. This would have enabled them to thoroughly assess the development applications, and would have been extremely valuable in helping to make the City's case to the OMB. An Area Plan would have been a clear demonstration that the development proposals in question did not fit with the City's planning policies. Why didn't City planners have an Area Plan for the WQWT prior to the development applications? The short answer is that the planning department is significantly underfunded, with many unfilled vacancies. Moreover, in a disturbingly ironic twist, much of the staff the planning department does have is kept busy dealing with OMB challenges. According to various estimates, City planners spend somewhere between one-third and one-half their time preparing for and testifying at OMB hearings. In other words, planners do not have time to create Area Plans because they are dealing with the OMB, and the absence of Area Plans makes it more likely that developers will be able to make successful appeals to the OMB.

The OMB is a rather curious legislative artifact. It was originally called the Ontario Railway and Municipal Board, and when it was established in 1897, one of its primary functions was to oversee the development of an intercity railway network. In its current form, the OMB is an anomalous institution – most large cities outside of Ontario retain ultimate authority over planning and zoning decisions taken within their own boundaries. Internationally renowned architect and urban designer Ken Greenberg, who is based in Toronto, finds the existence of the OMB troubling: 'This is a unique institution, to my knowledge. There's nothing like it anywhere else in Canada, there's certainly nothing like it in any jurisdiction I have worked in … The city basically doesn't make decisions about planning, because those decisions can be and are regularly countermanded by the OMB.' This, he says, 'casts a pall over all of the discussions of planning issues, and shapes what City planners do in this city, how they spend their time ... and causes [them] to feel that at any moment somebody's looking over their shoulder who's going to reject their advice.'

This pall isn't just felt in Toronto's planning department: there's a trickle-down effect that filters all the way down to the grassroots level. Because the public knows that the OMB can and routinely does overturn decisions made by the municipal government, there's a certain degree of cynicism and a sense of futility that is often attendant upon efforts to engage with City Council. After all, what good is it to convince your community council that a certain development doesn't fit in with your neighbourhood if the OMB is going to overrule the City a few steps down the line?

Just as significant as these two factors – the absence of an Area Plan and the power of the OMB – in the final outcome of the WQWT decision was the lack of community consultation on the part of the developers prior to drawing up their applications and submitting them to the City. Because there is no require- ment that developers conduct such consultations, they almost never do, and the net effect of this is to significantly ratchet up tensions surrounding contentious development projects. By the time the community is brought into the discussion (after the development application has been filed and before Council votes on it), developers are already wedded to their carefully drawn plans, in which they have invested considerable time and resources. The developers are therefore disinclined to make any significant changes, even if there are aspects of the devel- opment the community finds deeply unpalatable, and the community is inclined to feel itself under siege because it is presented with a complete, ready-to-go development proposal that it had no role in shaping.

The solution, of course, would be to engage the local community much earlier in the process, by requiring developers to consult before submitting preliminary applications to the City. This would amount to a fundamental change in the planning process, forcing revisions to be made to the City's bylaws and, quite possibly, to the provincial Planning Act.

While the politicians currently in office have expressed no commitments in this regard, some city councillors are trying to implement pre-application consultation processes in which they can impress upon developers who wish to build in their wards that the approval process will be significantly expedited if they undertake this consultation voluntarily and ahead of time. One downtown councillor in particular, Adam Vaughan (Ward 20), is known for getting developers to sit down with local residents prior to filing their applications.

Vaughan, in consultation with community organizations and members of the development, architecture, design and planning communities, has developed a robust, community-oriented process for development in his ward. One important component of this process is that any information he receives from developers about projects they are considering is immediately released to the public. Developers do not engage in a private process of consulting with the councillor's office before releasing their plans to the community, as happens in many other wards. Another component of the process is the creation of development checklists, which have been prepared by residents in each neighbourhood and detail the kinds of projects that would be welcome in the neighbourhood, as well as others that local residents feel are a poor fit. This means that a developer who is considering a project in Vaughan's ward knows from the outset what parcels of land and what kinds of developments are most promising, and which will raise the ire of the community and face strong resistance.

OMB hearings are costly and time-consuming, and Vaughan has done a good job of convincing developers that genuinely responsive, early consultations are preferable to drawn-out public battles. It's an admirable approach, and one that's been effective so far, but its success is entirely contingent on the determination of an individual councillor who happens to be interested in planning issues, yet who possesses no formal powers to compel the developers to comply with his requests for pre-application consultations. Which is to say that it's working, but it isn't a systematic solution unless it becomes systematically adopted.

Early consultation is not enough, however. For a planning process to truly engage with the local community, that community must be able to do more than simply express its views on a proposal – views that may or may not be taken into account by actual decision-makers. Rather, the community itself needs to become a decision-maker. There are a variety of models for this, both elsewhere and in Toronto's own history. New York City has fifty-nine community planning boards, for instance, each responsible for a designated part of the city. Each board is composed of up to fifty active members of the community who serve in a volunteer capacity. All applications for zoning variances must be reviewed by the relevant community board, and the board's position must be considered when the City makes its final decision on these applications. This gives communities not just a voice, but a (literal and metaphorical) seat at the table. Likewise, during the 1970s, planning decisions were made by a body called the City of Toronto Planning Board, comprised of a combination of politicians and appointed citizens. The board was abolished in the early 1980s in an attempt to reduce bureaucracy – though the success of that attempt is obviously questionable.

Under the current provincial Planning Act, the mechanisms for community engagement are organized by – and take place under the auspices of – municipal governments. In other words, communities are taken to have a voice in planning via their elected representatives, and while members of the public can make written submissions to City Council, Council is not required to accommodate those submissions in its decisions. As a result, says Toronto's former

Dina Graser, chair of PPT

chief planner Paul Bedford, 'most community groups here feel that they don't an effective way into having their voice heard at City Hall.' Bedford is a strong proponent of a return to some form of a Toronto planning board, as is Ken Greenberg. Both are also admirers of the community planning boards in New York.

People Plan Toronto is an organization that advocates for increased community participation in urban planning, and was born out of Active 18. PPT is, like just about everyone I spoke with, in favour of drastic reform to the planning process, but also devotes considerable energy to helping communities successfully navigate the existing system. Until any reforms are made, says PPT chair Dina Graser, knowledge truly is the most powerful tool available to those who want to engage more deeply in the planning process.

Over the past couple of years, PPT has networked with other community groups who have been dealing with their own development challenges, and has been putting together a set of resources to help interested citizens understand how to navigate planning decisions. PPT also worked with City staff to try to address some concerns about the zoning bylaw that was passed by the City in September 2010, tackling changes to built-form and other regulations that may noticeably alter how neighbourhoods feel at street level.

It's this kind of community work – the careful accumulation of information, the demystification of processes long deemed obscure by an overwhelmed public – that is slowly shifting the conversation about urban planning in Toronto, equipping residents with the ability to play a more active role in shaping their communities. It needs now to be matched by changes in official processes, so those residents can not only intervene more effectively in cases where they have concerns, but also contribute to a vibrant, participatory, city-building culture and play an active role in shaping their own communities.

Get involved

peopleplantoronto.org/

ward20.ca/districts.php: Adam Vaughan's community mapping project in Ward 20, a great example of how to engage citizens early in the planning and development process

I have acquired many debts of gratitude in researching this essay. For their time and insight, I thank Paul Bedford, Nicolas Fraser, Dina Graser, Ken Greenberg, Carole Goyette, Abdirizack Hersi, Carmen Smith, Nicole Swerhun, Cindy Wilkey and Margie Zeidler.

Hamutal Dotan moves to a different part of Toronto every few years and rediscovers the city each time. She writes about urban affairs, food policy and local culture, and is the senior editor of *Torontoist*.

Catherine Porter
The boxer
A guide to getting in the ring with City bureaucracy

It's midnight on a foggy November weeknight, and I'm out of my warm bed, flooding the Dufferin Grove rink with Jutta Mason.

We're breaking the rules. That much is for sure. That's Mason's modus operandi. She's been breaking City rules for fifteen years, which is why – in part – the Dufferin Grove rink house behind us has been transformed from the stinky, barren locker room you'll find beside most rinks in the city into a buzzing community hub, offering two-dollar bowls of split pea soup and boisterous games of sueca by the wood stove every afternoon.

Whenever a City staff person tells her, 'We can't do that because ... ' Mason hears, 'Do it yourself,' hence here we are, dressed in oversized jackets and rain boots instead of pyjamas, at midnight, flooding the rink.

Mason has convinced the City to open her local skating rink a week earlier than last year. For there to be skating, however, there needs to be ice, and she thinks that a midnight spray – when the sun isn't up to melt the ice as quickly as it forms – is the best strategy. Of course, no one at the City agrees.

'The $64,000 question,' she says, yanking at the industrial hose with her canary-coloured mitts, 'is how do you make bureaucracy work.'

I should add here that Mason is a sixty-three-year-old grandmother. And she doesn't skate.

Just to inspire you.

'The conundrum of bureaucracy is the problem of our times,' Mason continues, 'not just for the people outside it, but for the people working in it.'

Bureaucracy is not something I thought about much before working, with neighbours, to start a farmers' market in my neighbourhood. At our first meeting at City Hall, there were eighteen City staffers from four different departments in the room.

I don't suppose most people think much about bureaucracy, at least until they are inspired to change something in the city. Then they become intimately familiar with it – often in unpleasant and frustrating ways.

Take Cindy Rozeboom. Her idea for change was a ten-day arts fair across a stretch of Danforth Avenue. Art installations in abandoned lots and empty storefronts, participatory sculpture, graffiti demonstrations, musicians playing on street corners, silhouettes in street planters, exhibits in stores. Fairly ambitious. But she used to be in charge of marketing for the Fringe of Toronto Theatre Festival, with hundreds of plays across the city. How hard could ten days down sixteen blocks be?

Very hard, it turns out.

There were four city councillors to deal with and four separate City departments that didn't communicate with one another. What they communicated to her – at first – was a lot of 'can'ts.'

You can't put art up in empty storefronts, a City right-of-way staffer told her, as it would cause too much traffic on the sidewalk. You can't leave a sculpture in a park for all ten days, a permit officer told her, as the bylaw limits permits to three days. You can't put things in the City planters, she was told, but no one could tell her who was in charge of the planters. (Some are overseen by the City's forestry crews, while local business improvement groups tend to others, it turns out.)

The parks department and City licencing departments have different rules for permits. Neither informed her of that. She found out when one permit was rejected because of the difference between the departments.

Cindy Rozeboom

She was a boxer fighting a ghost in the ring.

'It was a nightmare,' she says. 'The frontline people, their first answer to everything is no and why you can't do things. It takes a lot out of you. It demoralized me.'

Now, if she'd only had a 'Toronto Bureaucracy for Dummies' handbook – something that laid out every department, what they do, who they are and how to work through them to accomplish what you want to get done. Or a mentor – some wily community activist who knows the system well and has run a similar event – to draw a map for her.

Imagine a community activist resource centre on the ground floor of City Hall. It would be a place where you could drop in, tell a librarian your idea and be directed towards resources, experts, case studies, maybe even professors at universities who are into just that stuff. Wouldn't that be great?

The closest thing I could find to this was the City's civic engagement office, which is way up in a tower and really just one person's desk. Good luck finding it. While she has put out some nifty 'how-to' community guides on things like hosting an all-candidates debate, her real mandate is to train City staff on ways to engage the public, but not to actually engage the public herself.

'That's what a councillor is supposed to do,' Councillor Adam Vaughan said when I described my dream community activist resource centre to him. Why bureaucratize a system meant to help navigate bureaucracy? he asked. Good point. But not all councillors are like Vaughan, who prides himself on helping community-builders make changes in his ward, and even community-minded councillors don't always like their community's ideas. What if your great scheme is a bike lane and your councillor is on the record saying anyone who bikes on a major street deserves to be hit by a car (i.e., Rob Ford)?

Cindy Rozeboom's local councillor was Case Ootes.

'Case Ootes never phoned me back. He never returned any of my emails,' she says. 'Not one.'

Then what?

The next best thing to a community activist resource library, I thought, was talking to some successful Toronto community activists and learning how they have managed to battle bureaucracy. I've chosen three with whom, as a fellow community activist, I'm particularly besotted right now. They've each done different things – ranging from the local to the municipal. And all three have been incredibly successful.

Since I've already introduced her, I'll continue with Rozeboom, a mother of two in her mid-forties whose day job is doing PR for the Scarborough Arts Council. Her idea was to get people engaged with their neighbourhood and their neighbours, through locally created art. The neighbourhood in question was the gritty end of the Danforth, where the Starbucks have petered out into Italian soccer clubs and the clothing boutiques carry exclusively second-hand stuff. It's where I live.

What Rozeboom pulled off was incredible. She transformed a drab parade of rundown and empty stores into a colourful, interesting, exciting strip.

The barren double lot near my house that has been empty since the owner allegedly set fire to his hardware store nine years ago became a place of birth, with figures bursting from the earth, and a string of flags – painted by local kids – fluttering above them. The fence behind a bleak parking lot was adorned with a giant purple horse and the word 'glue,' to remind passersby that this was once the site of an abattoir. There were paintings in store windows and on the walls inside, forcing you to step in.

It made me envision what our neighbourhood could be like all the time.

All created by one person, working late at night for one and a half years, after returning from work, feeding her family and putting her kids to bed.

But it almost didn't happen, because of bureaucracy.

Three weeks before the fair was to start, Rozeboom finally learned the cost of her permit for the use of one city park for three short events – one of them a community parade. It had taken weeks of back-and-forth with the parks-event-permits person, who had explained there were no longer set permit rates – rates were now tailored to each event, depending on the space and park and time. She couldn't give an estimate until she saw the completed plan. The final cost: $1,200.

A week later, Rozeboom was hit by another unexpected bill: $750 for a licence.

'No one told me about a licencing fee,' she says, incensed. 'That's literally coming out of my daycare cheque.'

In the end, Councillor Sandra Bussin came to the rescue. The parks permit was waived and the licencing fee slashed to $75.

Rozeboom was grateful. But the near-disaster simply underscored the arbitrary nature of what she calls Toronto's 'big tangled mess of bureaucracy.'

Next year, it might be easier for her. But it might not. The rules change at City Hall all the time, as do the people implementing them. Two years ago, the parks department was flat-out against bake ovens. Now they are for them.

'Just because one person says no, it doesn't mean there aren't ways around it,' Rozeboom says.

Her advice: build relationships with other groups in your neighbourhood. Like the residents' association and business improvement area. Those endorsements, she says, make you 'seem valid' in the eyes of many at City Hall.

Second, go up the chain. Find out who is in charge of the department and go straight there, rather than dealing with underlings. People with power can override rules. People below them can feel power only in applying those rules.

Finally, she says, make sure you have lots of support – people who will dress your wounds, squirt water in your mouth and convince you that you're winning a worthy fight before pushing you back into the ring.

Those are all guidelines Devon Ostrom also swears by. He is the brain behind the city's new billboard tax. A quiet, unassuming artist, Ostrom came up with the idea eight years ago. It went like this: billboards are ugly. They clog public space to convince us to buy things. Why not tax them for that privilege, and use that money to fund public art? He called it the Beautiful City billboard fee. City Council finally approved it in early 2010.

The story of the Beautiful City campaign is inspiring in many ways. Hundreds of young artists took on City Hall and learned how to lobby: they paid for Environics polls with painted canvasses, they met with the residents' associations of wards with intransigent councillors in the hopes they would apply the right pressure to flip a vote, and they often arrived at Council meetings with a laptop and internet link, so 4,000 people would be alerted, for example, that Councillor Norm Kelly was trying to exempt electronic billboards.

'There were sixty calls to his office before he finished his speech,' says Ostrom.

A whole other chapter should be written on that organizational flow chart – i.e., how do you mobilize sixty people to call an office in a matter of minutes? Ostrom is thinking about teaching a course on lobbying for activists. I hope he does.

Throughout the trajectory of his campaign – innumerable public consultations, hundreds of meetings with councillors and all the levels of committees – Ostrom became intimately familiar with the power of the city's bureaucracy to influence the outcome.

Near the end of the campaign, a single word change silently appeared on the proposal to go before Council: 'funding' was replaced with 'offset,' meaning the new money brought in by the tax would replace the current arts funding rather than boost it.

Where did that come from? He still doesn't know.

'Bureaucracy can kill,' he says. The flip side, though, was that a bureaucrat alerted him to the change.

Over the years, Ostrom has sought out sympathetic people inside the system. They've become his guides around blockages and red flags to problems.

That's a key, he thinks, to success at City Hall. 'If you get good relationships with civil servants, you are halfway there,' he says. 'Council can wiggle and waffle, but if you can get the bureaucracy to buy in, it's very hard to stop that beast once it's going.'

His other ringside rules? Make sure you are learning stuff and

Devon Ostrom

having fun, and don't dismiss your opponents – listen to them. 'It's important to hear what people's concerns are,' he says. 'There's something to be said for not looking at people as enemies right away. People open up channels you don't think will open, and most of the time they have legitimate concerns. Things get stronger if you can at least listen to what they have to say.'

Jutta Mason at the Dufferin Grove Park rink

Now for the woman in the canary mitts, hauling the industrial hose around Dufferin Grove ice rink: Jutta Mason.

For the past fifteen years, her mission has been to build community spaces. She's been very successful at it. (Before Dufferin Grove, she spearheaded the revitalization of Campbell Park, and later helped to overhaul its rink, at Dupont and Lansdowne.)

Two decades ago, Dufferin Grove was a scruffy park with drug dealers, a hollow concrete rink house and a lonely skating rink. It was not a community park.

Go by there most summer nights now, and you'll find families cooking meals over campfires, two wood-burning bake ovens churning out bread and pizzas, a café serving soup and cookies, and maybe even a play put on by the local theatre troupe, Clay and Paper, which has a clubhouse in the park. Neighbours gather here every Friday for a community supper.

The activity doesn't stop in the winter. Neighbours come to the rink house, eat a bowl of soup, take a spin on the ice – some renting skates for two dollars an hour – then settle down to read their kids a book by the wood stove with a cup of hot cocoa. It's a day's outing. And it's not by chance.

Mason was behind most of this. But it happened organically, in steps: first, windows in the rink house, then a wood stove, a grant for a kitchen, a donation of fifty pairs of skates from the National Hockey League Players' Association and a lending program.

She gleaned her rule of thumb from a former City manager,

An excerpt from *Cooking with Fire in Public*, a handbook by the Friends of Dufferin Grove Park on barbecues and bake ovens in parks

If picnic tables, drinking fountains or trash baskets are lacking, call your local city councillor and tell her/his assistant the problems. (You can get the number from the phone book or the municipal website.) Follow this up with an email or letter itemizing the problems in writing and ask that this list be forwarded to the Parks Department person in charge of that specific park. Ask the councillor to let you know what the Parks Department response was.

If the problems are not fixed in the park within two weeks, call the councillor's office back and ask why there's a delay.

If there is a good reason for the delay (for example, that four picnic tables are in the shop for repainting and will be returned tomorrow, or that the plumber has ordered a new part for the drinking fountain and will be installing it in two days), ask your city councillor for the phone number of the park supervisor and call her/him. Emphasize how glad you are that they are taking action and mention that there is a planned neighbourhood picnic in the park four days hence, when all the improvements will be fully appreciated by many concerned neighbours. If you want to give an additional little boost, mention that you are planning to invite the city councillor to this barbecue. Normally this news will help ensure the repaired items are delivered on or before schedule, rather than two months later.

---

she says. 'He said there are two rules for working with bureaucracy: start small, and use the rules against themselves.'

She and some neighbours were keen to build an old-fashioned community bake oven in the park. Parks staff told them fires weren't permitted in the park. But, combing through parks-and-recreation brochures, they found there was a policy encouraging heritage activities in parks. What's more historical than baking bread in a community oven?

It worked.

If there is no good reason for the delay in the park improvements you requested, go to your park and get out your camera. Take some pictures, of exposed nails or broken sections in picnic tables or benches, of trash on the ground with no evidence of trash baskets (or overflowing trash baskets), of broken water fountains, and of any other ugly or dangerous thing you happen to come across. When the pictures are developed, take a pair of scissors and cut off the empty bits in the pictures and fit all the remaining pieces into a nice little photo collage. Such a collage can visually concentrate the problems you're talking about in a way that gets through to people. Take this photo collage to your neighbourhood cut-rate colour xerox place and get them to print about ten copies. Mail copies to the Park Department manager whose area includes your park (you can find out his/her name and address, and all other names you need, from your city councillor's office)

• the policy/planning director responsible for 'park furniture,' and
• the city councillor.

If you're feeling very pessimistic, you could also mail copies to the director of the Parks Department and to the urban correspondents at your city newspapers. In your cover letter, mention the date when you began to ask for these problems to be fixed, and also mention, at the bottom, who else got a copy of the collage. Then take at least four of the remaining photo collages and post them at the park, with a little sign that says, 'If you think we deserve better than this, please call your city councillor

'If they can't let you do something for one reason, see if you can find a better reason, like working with youth,' she says.

Another rule she's learned over the years, she says, is follow-up. Many good ideas die in endless 'More Research' files.

'Bureaucracy rests on the principle no one follows up,' she says. 'You can fight City Hall with follow-up.'

But sometimes that doesn't work either. And sometimes, she's found, you just have to do it yourself. The wall, for example. There used to be concrete walls dividing the rink house into

---

at _____.' Point out these pictures to others in the park (have some pieces of paper with the city councillor's phone number in your pocket, to hand out) when you're in the park walking your dog or playing with your kid or checking to see if you can bring the family for a barbecue yet.

A 'slum park picnic'
Up to this point all the park-fixing suggestions made here have actually been tried, with success. We never had to go the next step. But if you still haven't got action within a week, you could try something like this (just one idea, not tested): Actually have the barbecue you threatened to have. Invite all your friends and put up signs in the park and the neighbourhood, also inviting any other park users to a potluck. Title the event something like 'a slum park picnic.' Emphasize that people should bring:
• bottled water, since your park is unable to provide a working drinking fountain
• their own chairs, since there are not enough picnic tables
• bandaids, disinfectant, and hammers, since the picnic tables that exist may have protruding nails
• a small spray can of paint, to cover over the graffiti
• garbage bags, since the City puts out insufficient trash bins.

Accompany your slum barbecue invitation to the city councillor with a nice package containing a bottle of water, the bandaids, the disinfectant, the hammer (you can ask for it back later) and a trash bag. If you like, you

---

smaller change rooms. Mason and her team proposed they come down. That would cost $8,000, the bureaucrats said. Who has $8,000? So, late one Saturday night, Mason et al. crept in and dismantled one.

'It's really easy to take down concrete blocks,' she says. 'You and I could do it tonight, but let's not.'

And the reaction? 'It's often been my experience when you do something like that, bureaucracy laughs. They find it very droll. They are so much struggling with the rules too.'

could also invite the Parks Department director, with the same kind of accompanying gift bag. Make some phone calls and spend some extra time in your park beforehand, to tell your neighbours that this is an important chance for them to make a point and have some fun as well. Chances are, if you pick your time well and give a week's notice, you'll get a good crowd. (If you know any clown or other children's performer who would be willing to come, advertise this on your invitation. If you're ambitious or inspired, also advertise garbage bag races, nail-hammering contests, water-bottle-balancing dances, and other foolish fun.) Whether you create a neighbourhood party that becomes an annual event – great fun just for being so peculiar – or you just get a small group of odd-sock neighbours who all bring day-old doughnuts for their potluck contribution, chances are the Parks Department will fix up your park's picnic facilities very soon. You'll have made so much fuss that it will be easier to address the problems than to continue to hear from you. So that would be one good outcome. The other is, doing this kind of in-your-face activism can give you a good chance to have a giggle. And if the officials who are getting your gift packs have a sense of humour, it may be that they'll laugh too.

From *Cooking with Fire in Public*, by the Friends of Dufferin Grove Park. The full brochure is available at www.dufferinpark.ca. Scroll down to the image of the yellow cover and click to download the PDF.

That doesn't mean, though, she thinks you should go out of your way and befriend bureaucrats like Ostrom did. Those allies are unreliable. They often move. Friendships can be restrictive. What if you disagree with your friend the bureaucrat and speak out against a policy? Are you double-crossing him?

'It's important to be polite and reasonable but not too friendly,' she writes in her delightful pamphlet *Cooking with Fire*, ostensibly about cooking in parks, but really about transforming them into community centres. 'Being friendly may take you in the direction of comfortable talk but not in the direction of action.'

Three activists, three different sets of advice. Where does that leave us?

Scratching our heads a bit.

What Mason does agree on is the fun part. If the battle is just that, a fight, then you will never win. You have to make it enjoyable.

Here's what I've learned in my foray into civic activism. It's like childbirth – painful at times, but ultimately so enchanting you forgive the harder moments, maybe even forget them. Once you've succeeded, you're hooked. You want more. Community empowerment is addictive.

I will always remember that first day our farmers' market opened – after all the scraps over street widths and tree locations, handwashing stations and traffic monitors. (I spent most of that first summer with my baby strapped to my chest and an orange vest draped over us both, stopping cars from coming down the street where farmers were parked.)

It was brilliant and sunny, and, despite all our fears, people came in droves, crowding the sidewalk with their wagons overflowing with basil plants and honey jars. Behind the farmers was a hill, rolling down towards the park. A whack of kids were doing somersaults down it while their parents shopped.

My heart felt like it would explode in my chest, I was so proud. I kept thinking: four of us did this together. Four little people, and we've made a difference to our neighbourhood.

Change can happen. It just takes work.

Get involved

dufferinpark.ca

artofthedanforth.com

beautifulcity.ca

toronto.ca/civic-engagement

Catherine Porter is an award-winning journalist with the *Toronto Star*. Now a columnist, she's also covered the environment and spent three years at City Hall. During her first maternity leave, she started a neighbourhood association that has livened her little east-end pocket of Toronto, with community movie nights, an annual craft fair and a weekly farmers' market. After years of recording activities, she finds its gratifying to be an activist herself. She is happily married and has two gorgeous kids.

Kelly Grant

The budget and you

How citizens could be involved in Toronto's budgeting process

'Come on down, baby!' That's the one-liner that got the most play at budget deputation night 2010, an annual charade where the public talks and councillors pretend to listen. 'Come on down, baby!' wasn't a saucy invitation to join the crowd at Toronto City Hall for a sensible chat about budgeting. It was the climax of a fight between a grey-haired resident in a suit and tie and Paula Fletcher, the Toronto-Danforth councillor and former leader of the Communist Party of Canada – Manitoba. He had chided the committee about spending too much. She had battered him with questions about what he would cut. Arts funding? Daycare? Breakfast programs for poor kids? How about Transit City, the plan to expand light-rapid transit into the inner suburbs? (Perhaps Councillor Fletcher should have asked Premier Dalton McGuinty that last question. He announced a few weeks after the meeting that his debt-wracked Liberal government would postpone $4 billion in funding for the lines.)

'My final question is,' Councillor Fletcher yelled, waving a pencil at the audience, 'there's many young people here tonight that haven't driven down here like you. Should we cut Transit City so they can't get down from North York and Rexdale and Malvern? Is that your *suggestion*? Is that your suggestion tonight? Called down here by the John Tory show?'

Acolytes of the politician-turned-Newstalk-1010-host cheered from the chamber's blue velour bleachers. Councillor Fletcher and the deputant screamed over each other. 'You should be fired,' he shouted. That's when Councillor Fletcher shot back, like a deranged Rod Roddy: 'Oh, come and run against me. Come on down, baby!' The clip spread like wildfire on YouTube, fanned by Tory and Toronto's other AM radio hosts. It summed up everything that's wrong with how City Council engages people on a simple question: How should Toronto spend its money? One man offered his two cents and got a buck's worth of insults from a woman whose salary he pays.

I was working on deadline in the City Hall press gallery the night of Councillor Fletcher's outburst, keeping an ear to the televised meeting while I typed a story about an earlier presentation from the Toronto Board of Trade. I chuckled when I heard Fletcher lose her cool, but it wasn't worth stopping the presses. First of all, Fletcher, a firebrand with close-cropped blond hair and a sultry singing voice that blows everyone away at the annual press gallery Christmas party, isn't known for her grace under pressure. I'd seen her temper rise before. More importantly, her behaviour didn't seem so grotesque if you'd watched the hours of presentations that preceded it. The YouTube clip was taken out of context. In reality, the night was worse, and the politicians weren't all to blame.

The crowd inside Viljo Revell's spaceship of a Council chamber could be crudely split into two camps, one with cap in hand, the other determined to block more public coin from being tossed in the upturned hat. The first group was made up largely of the arts groups and social service agencies that embark on the ritualistic trek to budget deputation night every year to ask for a larger increase to the budget of the Community Partnership and Investment Program, the City's grants program.

In 2010 the municipal government tried to freeze the CPIP budget. This was a generous move considering City Manager Joseph Pennachetti, Toronto's top bureaucrat, had ordered every part of the City to slash its budget by 5 per cent. But the grant recipients argued the freeze amounted to a cut; without an increase to cover inflation, they'd be forced to reduce staff or scale back service. One by one, they made their cases, playing videos of their clients singing, dancing and painting to drive home the point. Residents fretting about proposed cuts to child-care and Toronto's libraries joined them in asking for more cash. Meanwhile, Tory, who came within a few thousand votes of running the city in the 2003 election, finished broadcasting a special edition of his rush-hour show from City Hall's rotunda. He, too, urged people to come on down – to complain about city councillors raising property taxes and wasting money. 'A word of warning,' one of the anti-spending speakers said. 'We will not tolerate your racking up more and more debt for our children to pay for your mismanagement. If you are not up for the job, we will elect those who are.'

The budget committee members and other councillors who braved deputation night sat for hours while people excoriated them for spending too little and too much, for bankrupting their children's futures by proposing the closure of some libraries on Sunday afternoons and for bankrupting their children's futures by failing to extract the full 5 per cent cut from some departments, including the Toronto Public Library. The politi-cians didn't hear anything they didn't already know. The public didn't learn much about the budget. The only winner was YouTube. It was little wonder, then, that the committee room drained of performers on the second day of hearings, leaving the circus's usual closing act, the activist Raging Grannies, without an audience. As Budget Chief Shelley Carroll told me later, 'I understand the Raging Grannies showed up two hours late.'

As you might have guessed, I'm cynical about Toronto's token nods to public participation in the budget. The municipal government's budget is a horribly complicated document assem-bled by an army of pointy-headed accounting whizzes and presided over by a mayor and a seven-member budget commit-tee who have to make agonizing choices about what to axe. You couldn't pay me enough to do their jobs. That's why I elect them to do it for me. One of the most basic things we ask of our politicians is that they decide how best to spend our money.

The budget of a multi-billion corporation is a hairy beast. How hairy? First of all, Toronto has more than one budget. The City's water and solid waste departments run budgets entirely separate from the rest of the process. The capital budget, usually adopted in December, pays for hard infrastructure and major repairs such as paving roads, erecting bridges, buying buses and refurbishing buildings. It's here you'll find the City's debt. Anybody who talks about erasing that debt for good is harbouring the fantasy that Canada's largest metropolis can pay for all projects upfront, in cash. Mature cities whose books aren't engorged with development fees borrow money to pay for infrastructure.

But it's important to keep Toronto's capital debt at a manageable level because of how the interest on that debt affects the operating budget, the pot of money that means most to citizens' day-to-day lives. Imagine that pot as filled with a budgetary stew. Property taxes, raised by the municipality, are the main ingredient. In 2010, property taxes made up nearly 40 per cent of the budget. Grants and subsidies from Queen's Park made up 20 per cent. Dashes of federal subsidy, user fees, land-transfer and vehicle-registration taxes and a handful of other charges make up the rest. The recipe hasn't changed much since the megacity's birth in 1998. But the concoction has never been plentiful enough to feed everyone in town.

Toronto is perpetually broke. The City has a structural deficit, meaning that every year it would spend more than it collects if it didn't siphon money from rainy-day reserve banks, slash costs or receive an eleventh-hour bailout from Queen's Park. Arguments abound about how to close that structural gap for good, but even fierce critics of City spending can agree on its primary cause: downloading. At the same time as Mike Harris's Progressive Conservative government foisted amalgamation on Toronto, it monkeyed with who pays for what. (It didn't help that Mel Lastman, the megacity's first mayor, and his council passed property-tax freezes that the new metropolis could ill afford.) The province shouldered education funding, but made the City pay a share of social service costs, such as welfare. In a huge blow for Toronto, the province forced municipalities to pay the full freight of operating local transit, a departure from the long-held practice of splitting the cost fifty-fifty. The fact that the TTC can't pay its bills is one of the biggest reasons Toronto has a structural deficit. However, the City never runs an actual deficit. By law, it can't. So every year Toronto plays an elaborate game of close-the-gap. 'For the first term at least of Mel, the structure was more of political barter,' says David Soknacki, a budget chief from 2003 to 2006 who also worked on budgets under Lastman's budget chiefs, Tom Jakobek and David Shiner. 'Mel would say, "So here's the big envelope, Tom, go make it happen." So what he [Jakobek] would do is tap you on the shoulder in his very intense way and say, "I need your vote. What'll it take to get your vote?" It was about that explicit.'

Although the process evolved after the departure of Jakobek, best remembered as the villain of a huge computer-leasing scandal, budgeting in Toronto remained a messy affair. There were threats of 20 per cent property-tax hikes and service annihilation if the province didn't pony up. There were late-night camp-outs in the chambers as councillors cobbled together a balanced budget on the floor. Soknacki recalls the cheers and whirring of noisemakers when he banged the gavel on the 2006 budget around 2 a.m. 'You got punchy at the end,' he says.

The close-the-gap game changed fundamentally in 2008 when Mayor David Miller unveiled Toronto's first 'balanced budget.'

Now, instead of threatening the province and residents with extraordinary hardships in public, the City's finance gurus bridge the gap in private and unfurl a *fait accompli*. Tweaks are possible as the budget winds its way through committee – deputation night is one stop on the journey – but the fundamentals rarely budge.

The new approach enraged some of Miller's opponents on Council, along with activists such as journalist and professor Judy Rebick, who has written extensively about participatory budgeting. 'It's pathetic,' she said. 'The budgeting process from what I can see is less democratic under David Miller than it's ever been.' But there was barely a peep from the public.

The new system came about because Premier Dalton McGuinty's government wanted to deal with an 'adult government,' Councillor Carroll, budget chief during David Miller's second term, explains. 'Mature, mature, mature,' she says. 'That was the operative word.' Sick of Toronto shoving the province's toes into the flames every budget season, McGuinty asked that funding deals be worked out thoughtfully and privately, an approach that bore fruit when the province agreed to slowly take back the full cost of welfare from municipalities.

Councillor Carroll, a funny and sensible suburban mom, is a good soldier. She has led former mayor Miller's new system of closed-door budgeting, defending it at every turn. But as she prepares for what will likely be a stint in the political wilderness under the mayor's replacement, she tells me the secretive process was a mistake: 'Having used this system for four years, I see now that there is no way, no way we can do some of the kinds of sweeping changes in finance and governance that need to happen for twenty years from now.' Caroll has long argued that Toronto needs a wider selection of taxes to thrive as it grows, and insists that you can't ask residents to support new taxes if you shut them out of the budget process. 'It's even detracted from understanding that in a lot of ways we don't have problems,' she says. 'This is a great city to live in. That's being lost because they don't see some of the victories within a budget process.'

For instance, in 2010, Pennachetti, the City manager, morphed into Dr. No, wringing $172 million in ongoing savings out of the budget and producing a whopping $350 million surplus from 2009. But $100 million of that surplus was nailed down after budget day and unveiled at a crassly political press conference in Miller's office. Residents who had been told the City didn't have $208,000 to stave off closing twenty-seven libraries five Sundays a year were furious. 'In a closed process,' Carroll says, 'nobody believes any of it.'

How, then, can Toronto open its budget and let the public in, without bogging down the process with so many consultations it becomes unmanageable? Some partial answers lie in our own backyard: in a tiny storefront in Toronto's Corktown and the basement of a public-housing tower at Danforth and Greenwood.

The wee storefront is home to MASS LBP, an upstart public consulting company run by a squad of twenty-and thirty-some-things who manage to celebrate public participation without crossing into woolly-headed hippie territory. 'Our politics are haunted by a kind of phantom public which doesn't even exist,' says Peter MacLeod, the thirty-one-year-old political scientist who leads MASS. He blames the status quo partly on pollsters who catch people at dinner and ask them for opinions on subjects about which they know little. Someone who reflexively backs tough-on-crime policies might think otherwise with more information, MacLeod says. 'It's a caricature, but if you actually take that hard-bitten son-of-a-bitch and you sit him down with some kid who comes from a troubled family and has had none of the opportunities afforded to most people ... people change their minds pretty quickly.'

Creating that kind of opportunity during public consultation is MASS's raison d'être, MacLeod and four other MASS staffers tell me over wine and cheese in their office on a Friday evening. (The vino and snacks, leftovers from a visit with British embassy officials, aren't a regular indulgence, they say. I believe them after MacLeod tells me he and his staff all earn the same salary, $49,500 a year, and after a pack of raccoons start jostling inside the walls of their office.) MASS's method is unlike anything I've seen in my years covering public consultations. The company holds civic lotteries modelled loosely on the citizens' assemblies in British Columbia and Ontario that proposed new voting systems that were later turned down in referenda. When MASS is hired to consult the citizenry, it mails out invitations to thousands of people asking them to take part in forty hours or more of education and discussions before making recommendations. From those who reply, MASS picks a panel that roughly mirrors the area's demographics, weeding out meeting junkies and entrenched interests.

One of their projects especially intrigued me. The Northumberland Hills Hospital in Cobourg, about an hour east of Toronto on Lake Ontario, hired MASS last year to create and lead a citizens' advisory panel that would recommend cuts to the hospital, which was staring down a deficit for the third straight year. Its members would be asked to make tough choices about which of the hospital's programs were 'core' – essential and off the chopping block – and which were not. The final decision rested with the hospital board, but the panel's advice would be critical. For five Saturdays over the fall and early winter of 2009, twenty-eight ordinary, unpaid residents – a group reduced in the end to twenty-five by family emergencies – listened as the hospital's CEO, its vice-presidents of finance and patient services, nurses, doctors and others explained their slice of the hospital's money dilemma.

'I'd never seen anything like that before, where somebody asked for your opinion or input on something,' says panellist Pat Stanley, a well-spoken sixty-one-year-old retiree who moved to Cobourg from Toronto with her husband in 2002. On the first Saturday, she recalls, MASS instructed the twenty-eight strangers to stand up and arrange themselves according to geography, with one wall standing in for Lake Ontario and another for Rice Lake. 'That was just something to draw us together,' Stanley says. 'It helped, I think, make us realize that we came from all over the county but we came together for one reason: to help the hospital.' It also helped the panellists see that neither Cobourg, a town of 18,000, nor neighbouring Port Hope, home to just over 16,000, would dominate the panel and exacerbate local jealousies. 'Port Hope and Cobourg are like the Montagues and Capulets of Eastern Ontario,' MacLeod says. (One Port Hope panellist who was new to the area joked to me that he had to bring his passport to get into Cobourg.) In the end, the panel recommended banishing to the non-core category outpatient rehab, a diabetes prevention clinic and long-term and palliative-care beds – not because these services weren't valuable, but because the panellists felt they could be delivered outside an acute-care hospital. On the last day, panellists were exhausted but satisfied. 'I never thought I would have seen citizens hugging the administrator of a hospital before,' says Chris Ellis, MASS's director of business development. 'It was different from the ending of a town hall meeting, let's put it that way.'

The panellists with whom I spoke had mixed feelings about the experience. 'I went from relief to rage to exhaustion and, okay, back to renewed energy,' says Teresa Williams, a thirty-seven-year-old single mother and community legal worker who joined the panel to speak for her underprivileged clients. 'It was certainly not easy and in the end … well, it wasn't rewarding, right? Services were cut.'

By March of 2010 the board had followed much of the panel's advice, closing the outpatient rehab and diabetes education clinics and cutting eleven interim long-term care beds, seven complex-continuing-care beds and sixteen alternative-level-of-care beds in acute units. Consulting a small group of unpaid citizens through the panel in no way shielded the hospital board, or the Local Health Integration Network that controls the purse strings, from fierce public anger about the cuts. Taking away existing services will always be an unpopular proposition. But in this case, at least ordinary people helped make the calls. Their participation made a difficult situation better for the people of Port Hope and Cobourg.

Public participation is easier when you ask people to decide how to spend money rather than how to save it. Take Toronto Community Housing. For nine years, it has run the only real participatory budgeting program in the city.

The premise is simple: elected tenant representatives from public-housing complexes across the metropolis meet once a year to ask for the upgrades and repair jobs their buildings need most. But the total price tag of all the projects on the table exceeds the cash available. So the group takes a vote. The 2010 participatory budget allocation night – PB night for short – in Don Valley–Beaches began with a hot meal in the common room of Greenwood Towers, just north of the Danforth. Ceiling fans whirred and polite conversation buzzed as thirty-two tenant reps pulled up orange vinyl chairs to a long rectangular table and prepared to make their pitches. Bristol-board displays of stained carpeting, cracked walls and mouldy ceilings lined the walls like sad science-fair projects.

'Hello, everybody, and welcome to your Don Valley–Beaches allocation day,' said Mario Clementi, a TCH health promotion officer who worked the room like a gentle stand-up comic all night. 'Woooo!' the tenant reps responded, clapping and cheering. Clementi explained the rules. TCH had $413,869 to spend in their area. The thirty-two projects on the table totalled more than $500,000. Each rep would get ten votes, cast by secret ballot. Projects with the most votes would get funded. Those at the bottom of the list wouldn't.

Clementi and his assistants circled the room with a mic, offering each delegate two minutes to make a case. 'Our building is surrounding by a lot of gangsters. Unfortunately, it's really sad to say, a lot of crackheads,' said forty-year-old Bibi Shaw, who lives with her nine-year-old daughter in the Upper Beach. 'I try to go out the door in the morning and I don't know what's on the other side.' She wanted money to install security cameras in her TCH building at 520 Kingston Road.

'As you can see from the pictures, our building has less than zero curb appeal,' said thirty-five-year-old Leslie Reid as she showed off a photo of Astroturf duct-taped to the floor of the front entranceway to keep seniors from slipping on their way into 220 Eglinton Avenue East. The group whizzed through their pitches in just over an hour. When the votes were tallied, both Shaw and Reid were among the winners – but their divergent opinions of the process are proof participatory budgeting is no panacea.

'This is way better because they listen, they have the time, they take the time, it's not like we have to work around each other's schedules,' Shaw says. But Reid has two complaints. The project for which her building won funding the year before – new security cameras – still hadn't been completed, shaking her faith in the TCH's promises. And she knows the voting wasn't all about the merit of the project; the pitches were so quick because so many people planned to vote for their friends in the tight world of TCH tenant reps.

'People who were well-liked didn't get very many questions,' she says. 'People already knew who they were going to vote for.' The MASS and TCH models may not be perfect, but they provide encouraging local lessons in participatory budgeting. Toronto could also look to Chicago for inspiration on participatory budgeting. The Windy City is famous for a lot of things – cronyism and corruption spring to mind – but robust participatory democracy isn't one of them. In the spring of 2010, Rogers Park, a neighbourhood on Chicago's far north side, took a chance on a project that could help change the city's reputation. Local alderman Joe Moore decided to turn his 'menu money' – $1.3 million in discretionary cash – over to the first participatory budgeting experiment in U.S. history. With the help of a non-profit group called the Participatory Budgeting Project, Moore and dozens of community volunteers selected thirty-six community projects and put them to a vote. The process was rigorous. For example, volunteers walked every sidewalk in the neighbourhood to determine which sections were so badly damaged they deserved a place on the ballot.

In April 2010, more than 1,600 people over the age of sixteen, and regardless of citizenship status, voted to fund fourteen projects, including bike lanes, murals, community gardens and a massive sidewalk upgrade that received more support than any other proposal. 'Voter turnout exceeded everyone's expectations,' says Josh Lerner of Participatory Budgeting Project, which helped run the Chicago experiment. 'It's a more demanding act of participation than voting for just a person, which is pretty easy. This was asking people to seriously consider what the needs were for the ward.'

The alderman plans to do it all again next year.

The Rogers Park experiment wouldn't seem so revolutionary in Latin America and parts of Europe, where participatory budgeting is much more advanced than it is in North America. A Brazilian city called Porto Alegre was the pioneer. In 1989, the city began turning part of its budget process over to the people. It was so successful, the process has expanded to the point where as much as 20 per cent of the city's budget is decided through a year-long process of citizens' assemblies and plenaries.

Compared to Porto Alegre, Toronto has a lot of catching up to do. But the city could start with small steps on the path trodden by the MASS LBP, Toronto Community Housing and Rogers Park in Chicago.

A coalition of local community organizations is trying to do just that. The Toronto Open Budget Initiative – led by the Toronto Women's City Alliance and Social Planning Toronto – has set itself the ambitious goal of teaching ordinary citizens how City Hall spends their money, a task that would be much easier if City Hall let ordinary citizens in on the secrets of budget-making. 'What we're asking for is not revolutionary,' says Melissa Wong, a co-chair of TOBI whose group is seeking small but significant changes like public consultations before – not after – the budget is set. 'Nobody's really happy with the current process, so I think there's definitely space to change.'

In June 2010, TOBI helped get a motion to that effect passed at City Council, but the motion's tepid language – it boils down to a promise that the City manager will look into it – suggests it would take a crowbar to further open Toronto City Hall. Or, perhaps, a stick of dynamite. 'This is a scandal the way this works. There's no way that people can have any say. It's all decided before it goes to consultation,' Judy Rebick says. 'To me, you need to just blow it up.'

Get involved

masslbp.com

watsonblogs.org/participatorybudgeting

sites.google.com/site/torontoopenbudget

Kelly Grant is the Toronto City Hall bureau chief for the *Globe and Mail*. She has also covered crime, courts and politics for the *Windsor Star* and the *National Post*. Kelly practices participatory budgeting at home with her husband, Tom; yellow lab, Roxy; and their new addition, due in April 2011.

Jonathan Goldsbie
Permission impossible
Creating change outside the system

Friday, July 11, 2008, was the first time I memorized a TTC schedule for the particular purpose of *missing* a bus. It would have been unbearably awkward to be asked by the driver of the 31 Greenwood exactly what it was we were doing on top of the bus shelter with our ladders, flower planters and miniature white picket fences. Even though the explanation was as simple as 'creating a garden,' we weren't entirely confident that the Toronto Transit Commission would see it that way.

Two years earlier, the City of Toronto had gathered dozens of designers and architects to devise best practices for the city's next generation of 'street furniture,' a term that encompasses transit shelters, garbage bins, benches and postering kiosks, among other things. At the end of the charrette, the most common suggestions included designing for 'local involvement' ('the ability to involve the neighbourhood in adding art') and with 'green components' ('shelters with green roofs and solar powered lighting'). Yet innovation is not exactly the strong suit of either bureaucracies or billboard conglomerates, so in the end Toronto's street furniture wound up being a uniformly grey affair, both figuratively and literally.

That's when members of a few of the Toronto Public Space Committee's different campaigns – the Great Toronto Sidewalk Sale, a group fighting against placing transit shelters under the control of an advertising company; Art Attack, which uses art to reclaim the visual environment from corporations; and Guerrilla Gardening, which plants flowers in neglected corners of the public space – sprang into action. The TPSC's broad mission is to protect, enhance and celebrate Toronto's public realm; here we were trying to do all three.

Much like conceptual artists, activists have a responsibility to reveal the possible. That task becomes especially fun when ladders are involved. But politics shouldn't be a pretext for this sort of mischief; they should be its raison d'être. Context is key. Far from being anarchic, these projects are about doing government better than government does, and certainly better than businesses do it. It's about stepping outside the bounds of the designated channels, and perhaps even the law, but staying within the principles of a reasonable, just and good-humoured society.

Bureaucracy is frustrating. Well, duh. But it can also be empowering and amazing if you know how to wield it to your own advantage. This is what good politicians do.

Politicians are frustrating. Also duh. But the political system can be empowering and amazing if you know how to wield it to your own advantage. This is what good lobbyists do.

Successful activism often involves emulating the tactics and strategies of professional lobbyists in order to directly negotiate for legislative change with elected leaders. More often than not, this happens in the backrooms – some of the strongest public advocacy is almost inherently elitist, as it involves a degree of access that not everyone is equally able to obtain.

A lot of activist training involves attempts to distribute this privilege through the sharing of tips, tricks and methods for engaging with various power structures. This dissemination of knowledge is important and necessary. But a whole other category of civic action exists that is based on the simple principle of going out and doing shit – of being the change you want to see in the world. In these cases, it's a matter of functioning not within the system but just slightly around and outside its margins. It's about meddling with the public sphere directly, as an assertion of our individual and collective rights to shape our own environments.

Hence, for example, the TPSC's Guerrilla Gardening, whose motto is 'Vandalizing the city with nature.' It's both a celebration of grassroots investment in the public realm as well as a dare to authorities to oppose the thing it celebrates. Will the government take itself so seriously as to crack down on the unsanctioned planting of flowers? In Toronto, anyway, the answer has thankfully been no.

What happens when we raise the stakes a little by moving from guerrilla gardens to guerrilla infrastructure? That's what the Urban Repair Squad does. From 2005 to 2007, the URS took it upon themselves to install bike lanes on Toronto streets. *NOW Magazine* named them Toronto's best activist group of 2007.

In 2008, the URS expanded their repertoire to include DIY sharrows (chevrons that remind cars of the presence of cyclists) and bike boxes (designated spaces for bikes to stop ahead of traffic at red lights). On Sunday, January 25, 2009, the URS hit up all sixty-nine TTC stations, replacing standard stickers indicating the times that bikes are prohibited on the subway with new stickers indicating the times that bikes are allowed. The following morning, they used an email-spoofing service to send out an official-looking press release that appeared to come from the TTC itself: 'The Toronto Transit Commission announces it's [sic] new bike-friendly attitude for Toronto two-wheelers with the "Warm Welcome" campaign.' *NOW* mistook it for a genuine TTC initiative.

By moving street art and culture-jamming into the realm of municipal policy, the URS highlights the ineffectiveness and indifference of a lethargic civic government that continues to drag its heels on implementing simple changes that would tangibly benefit the safety and psyche of cyclists. It doesn't take years of public consultations, scores of staff hours and tens of thousands of dollars to construct a bike lane; all you need is a can of paint, a roller and maybe a stencil or two.

The Urban Repair Squad's mission statement, which appears in the sidebar of their blog, reads as follows:

- To encourage bicycling as an antidote to the poison that is car culture.
- To actively construct a positive future of what urban transportation could be by installing it NOW.
- To encourage citizens to reclaim ownership and stewardship of their urban space.
- To employ the concept of Critical Mass; encouraging cyclists to bond together and more safely take back their rightful place on the public roadways.
- Your city is broken. Don't wait for the bureaucrats to fix it. DO IT YOURSELF.

The URS is not reckless, and this is key to its credibility as an activist group. Its actions are careful and considered and render the urban environment more safe, not less. (The implicit message is that it is the government that is reckless by not doing these things itself.) Just as guerrilla gardeners claim stewardship of the public realm by beautifying it, the URS takes responsibility for the public realm by reconfiguring it to be more accommodating for all users. Everyone has an equal right to public space, and sometimes a little insistence is necessary.

One night each fall, the 'urban bliss disseminators' of Newmindspace set themselves up in the pedestrian plaza at the southwest corner of King and Bay streets and hand out between 1,200 and 2,000 glow sticks. The thin tubes – perfect for twisting into necklaces – come in three fluorescent colours: one represents the team north of King, another represents the team south of King and a third designates the volunteer referees.

This annual game of Capture the Flag has been taking place in Toronto's Financial District since 2006. The contest's physical boundaries are typically Richmond Street to the north, Front Street to the south, University Avenue to the west and Yonge Street to the east, with King Street serving as the dividing line between territories. Players must venture onto the opposing team's turf, locate the flag and bring it back over to their own side – all without being tagged.

With several hundred players stalking about at street level, crossing over into enemy terrain, let alone pinpointing the flag, is more than a little difficult. The trick, therefore, is to take advantage of the subterranean labyrinth that connects all of the buildings in the area. Nominally overseen by the City of Toronto, the underground PATH network's individual sections are owned and operated by whichever property management company happens to be responsible for the bank tower above. This means there are several security companies that don't have a coordinated response to Capture the Flag. Certain properties inevitably lock themselves up – both above and below ground – and shoo out anyone possessing a telltale glow stick. For the players, it's just another obstacle in a real-life video game that becomes more challenging as the evening wears on.

This game of Capture the Flag is a reminder of the nature of the hybrid spaces in the city that are privately owned but intended to be accessed by the public. The Financial District is unusual as downtown neighbourhoods go in that it's virtually abandoned at night, but during Capture the Flag, its empty – yet safe – expanses are playfully redefined as the blurring of public and private is pushed to an absurd extreme.

The objective of the exercise is not explicitly political, but that's part of the appeal. Kevin Bracken and Lori Kufner have been holding events under the Newmindspace banner since Bracken came to Toronto for university in 2005. Stemming from a raver-inspired sense of prolonged adolescence, Newmindspace's games and celebrations (they also hold annual pillow fights and 'bubble battles' in both Toronto and New York) are especially subversive in that they impart a sense of ownership of the urban landscape to open-minded teenagers who are mostly seeking an evening of cheap fun. Much as raves have traditionally involved the reclamation of abandoned industrial sites, Newmindspace's events reconceive the city as an under-appreciated playground that most of us don't recognize we have the freedom to use. Newmindspace also makes a point of declining offers of corporate sponsorship. In a city in which it is typical for large-scale events to wedge a bank's brand into their titles, Newmindspace shows that fun can be brought to you without the co-operation of big financial institutions.

Office buildings are hardly the only off-limits spaces ripe for infiltration. In May 2007, the TPSC carried out an 'Art Attack' against Astral Media Outdoor. Three years earlier, the billboard company had struck a deal with the City's Parks and Recreation division to place information kiosks in parks. Of course, providing public information is not what an advertising company is in business to do, so two of the three sides of each pillar consisted of outwardly curving, brightly illuminated billboards, while tucked away on a third, concave side was a map. Astral – with the City's full support and encouragement – had found a way to get around the bylaws prohibiting billboards in public parks.

Astral installed twenty-four of the pillars in the summer of 2005, at the commencement of what was ostensibly a five-year 'pilot.' By 2007, they were already falling apart: the maps faded (even as the ads were regularly refreshed), the audio functions operated inconsistently and the pocket-size-map dispensers would often malfunction. At the same time, City Council was in the process of awarding Astral the aforementioned street furniture contract, granting the company control over a far broader range of infrastructure, and for a twenty-year period. The new contract would bring the total number of ad pillars to 145, with the additional ones being placed directly on sidewalks. (A January 2008 *Toronto Star* audit of the fifteen downtown info pillars found the items to be in 'lamentably poor order'; a follow-up a year and a half later discovered that little had changed.)

On Monday, May 21, 2007, members of the TPSC gathered on the steps of the University of Toronto's Victoria College to create art. We cut large rolls of brown kraft paper into sheets to match the dimensions of the pillars' ad faces, which we obtained from the company's website. With markers and crayons, we sketched clouds, flowers, trees, a polka-dot octopus, as well as some more pointed messages like 'You are NOT what you consume.' On Tuesday, we converged in Nathan Phillips Square and divided up the locations to blitz, information also obtained from the company's website. We made it to all twenty-five – from the Beaches to North York – in a few hours. (The TPSC's adhesive material of choice is always tape. We prefer a passive-aggressive approach to culture-jamming, so that our actions don't cause damage and are easily reversible, yet still make a point. It allows us to straddle a line between organizational legitimacy and merry pranksterism.)

On the Thursday following the papering, I was sitting in Council chambers awaiting the vote on the street furniture contract when a friendly councillor warned me that we had allegedly been captured on camera and that Astral was looking to sue us for 'damages' – the revenue ostensibly lost for the period during which the ads were obstructed. He advised me to have a lawyer on standby.

I earnestly sent a Facebook message to *NOW Magazine*'s Jenny Yuen, who had joined us for the event, to request that her article not identify any of the individuals involved. (The TPSC, being an unincorporated entity, could not itself be sued.) The rumoured legal threat became the subject of Yuen's *NOW* piece, and she got an Astral spokesperson to state on the record that the company had no intention of going after us. And that was that.

After several months of more traditional advocacy against the street furniture contract, the experience of the Art Attack was a cathartic one. Although we had been unsuccessful at persuading Council to turn down the millions of dollars Astral was promising, it was nice to remind ourselves that the city's public spaces don't have to slip from our grasp, and that a handful of individuals relying on donations could still fashion themselves into worthy adversaries of those who believe that the citizens of this city are merely consumers.

On April 27, 2010, street artist Posterchild went after an info pillar on the University Avenue median, just north of Dundas Street. He replaced the advertisements not with art, but with useful information, relevant to both tourists and residents, about the nearby Canada Life Building, and how to read its famous, if somewhat mysterious, weather beacon. He created one panel in English, another in French. He didn't merely cover up the ads – he opened the structure and slipped his creations in their place. A public service.

Four months later, Posterchild was one of sixty artists who took part in TOSAT, the Toronto Street Advertising Takeover. Led by New York City's Jordan Seiler, who had previously undertaken similar campaigns in his hometown, TOSAT was a large-scale art assault on Pattison Outdoor, the company that – in raw numbers – has the most illegal ad structures in Toronto, according to IllegalSigns.ca, an advocacy group that researches billboards in Toronto.

Partly in response to the billboard industry's persistent and deliberate disregard for Toronto's signage rules, City Council had adopted a comprehensive new billboard bylaw in December

2009. Among other things, it included strong provisions for its own enforcement so that it would succeed where its predecessors had failed. But by summer 2010, there had yet to be any evident change in Toronto's visual environment, despite the estimation that upward of half of the city's 4,000 billboards were illegal.

And so TOSAT – a collaboration between Seiler's Public Ad Campaign and Torontonian Vanessa Butterworth's Duspa Corner Collective – in an act of guerrilla bylaw enforcement, unlocked approximately forty of Pattison's pedestal signs and replaced their ads with art. They also painted over the faces of nearly twenty ten-foot-by-twenty-foot billboards. The rationale was that if someone installs a structure in your living room without your consent, it's within your right to remove it or, failing that, to decorate it to your own taste.

Unlike with the New York Street Advertising Takeovers in April and October 2009, not a single participant in this action was arrested. The end goal of such an undertaking is the media reports. The TOSAT participants thoughtfully brought a couple of journalists along for the ride. Embedded reporters are sympathetic reporters; the resulting articles included quotes from civic officials who had to explain why it was taking them so long to go after illegal advertisements themselves. Rather than being portrayed as aggressive and spiteful, the TOSATers came across as ambitiously playful civil servants.

In a world without heroes, you have to be your own. That sentence is manifestly ridiculous (and possibly plucked from a movie trailer), but it's also sort of true. It's worth creating your own centre of gravity, your own brand, your own momentum. Don't try to mimic others. Do your own thing, be your own self and trust that other people want the world to be the same way you want it. This is much less a recipe for kamikaze insanity than it sounds; it's a plan for getting things done.

Activism is about the reclamation and possession of the institutions, spaces and rights on which we often have only a tenuous hold. It's about citizens' responsibility to guide society the way we want it to go. It's about keeping government accountable to the interests of the people for whom it's supposed to be working. In the last decade, Toronto has seen a resurgence of pride in and awareness of the urban landscape, and guerrilla activists are the ones who give concrete form to that love, the ones who put lofty democratic ideals into practice.

Don't ever feel locked out of a capacity to effect change, even when that may be the implicit purpose of most political establishments. Plant your own damn flowers, paint your own damn bike lanes and paper over the detritus strewn about your city by ad companies that have neither your forgiveness nor your permission. Be responsible and be smart. Run for City Council when you can and meddle with the civic bureaucracy when you can't. Pick your battles wisely, and pick your battles whimsically.

Get Involved

www.publicspace.ca

newmindspace.com

publicadcampaign.com/tosat

urbanrepairs.blogspot.com

bladediary.com

duspacollective.org

After years of being an activist who did journalism on the side, **Jonathan Goldsbie** is now a journalist who does activism on the side. He began doing advocacy work with the Toronto Public Space Committee in 2005 and became its chief campaigner in 2007, specializing in issues of outdoor advertising, street furniture, and public-space surveillance. As he became increasingly familiar with the back rooms and inner workings of City Hall, he began to write about it, first for *Torontoist* and then for *Eye Weekly* and *Spacing* magazine. He is now a municipal politics columnist at the *National Post*, and happily calls himself the paper's 'resident communist.'

Dave Meslin
illustrated by Marlena Zuber
Civic Engagement 101

Part 1: How does City Hall work?

City Hall can be a confusing place. It belongs to all of us, though, and it's important that we know how it works, and that we feel comfortable walking through its corridors. City Hall is where decisions are made that affect our streets, our parks and our services. Here is a brief overview of how these decisions are made, and how you can participate in the decision-making process and make sure your voice is heard.

Staff reports

City councillors make all the final decisions at City Hall, but most of the research, planning and writing leading up to votes at council is done by City staff. All initiatives at the City begin with a staff report, which can be triggered by a direct request from council or as a result of an existing plan like the Bike Plan or the Environment Plan. Staff reports include background information on the issue under discussion and, often, a recommendation from staff. Sometimes staff will consult with community experts or stakeholders while drafting a report. Sometimes this is the best opportunity to win a battle at City Hall. Influencing a staff report means you might win the fight before it even starts. Of course, to be able to influence a staff report, you have to know it's being drafted, which means staying in close contact with allies on staff. Remember: it's much easier to go to City Hall to support a staff recommendation than to oppose one.

Standing Committee and Community Council

Before a staff report goes to City Council, it goes to a smaller committee of councillors. It can go either to a community council meeting (comprised of local councillors from a region of the city) or one of the City's seven standing committees, such as the Parks and Environment Committee, which deal with specific areas of interest. The community councils and standing committees provide the most substantial opportunity for citizens to be heard at City Hall: at these meetings, any resident of the city can speak for five minutes about any issue. The presentation is called a 'deputation,' and it's your chance to express your opinion in front of councillors, City staff and the media. If you're

planning to make a deputation at a committee meeting, it's a good idea to bring out lots of your supporters to fill the room. But select only a handful of people to speak, and be sure they're each presenting different perspectives on the same issue, and relating them back to a consistent core message.

Public consultations

Substantial plans for new bylaws or development plans will often trigger a public consultation process, which is organized by City staff. These events are designed to present a recommendation (or a list of options) to the public and solicit feedback from residents. Unlike at the committee meetings, residents do not get five minutes to speak, and politicians don't tend to attend these events, so in some ways you have less voice here than you would at committee. On the other hand, deputants are sometimes completely ignored by councillors at committee, whereas City staff often do a better job of listening and incorporating all the voices into the next version of their report.

City Council

City Council is comprised of forty-four councillors and a mayor. They make all the final decisions, and can send reports back to staff, back to committee or back to further public consultations if they choose. Unlike community council or standing committee meetings, residents are not able to make public

deputations at City Council. But you can still get your message across visually, by wearing colourful T-shirts, buttons or hats that will identify you as a group. Signs are not permitted, and neither is clapping. However, if you can mobilize a critical mass of people, and encourage selective use of short bursts of applause, the speaker will bend the rules a bit for you. Politicians like applause, so having a large group in the council chamber can help push undecided councillors off the fence and onto your side of the issue.

Part 2: Turning ideas into action

I have an idea!

Every campaign starts with an idea or vision. Do you want a speed bump on your street? A new farmer's market in your community? Maybe you're concerned about a new development or a proposal coming out of City Hall. We all have opinions. Civic engagement is all about taking your ideas and opinions and pushing them further, developing them into a project or campaign. It's easier than you think! Here are the basic steps to organizing people in your neighbourhood for positive change:

Research

Get your facts straight. What is the history of this issue? How did it get to this point? Who are the key players? What's happening in other cities? Are there statistics you can gather? Have polls or surveys been done on this issue? How is it related to larger issues such as health, equality, culture and sustainability?

Build a team

You can't do this alone. (Okay, you probably can, but you might lose your mind trying.) You've got to pull a team together. Look for people who care about the issue, people who can work together, people you trust. Look for a variety of skills and backgrounds: design, writing, research, public speaking, business skills, fundraising, group facilitation, leadership, mediation, sense of humour.

Host a small meeting

Meetings can be fun! Bring your team together to give everyone a chance to meet, share ideas, brainstorm, strategize and delegate specific tasks. Always bring food and drinks to meetings. Host them in a quiet but relaxing location; avoid loud places like bars, but also avoid lifeless boardrooms with fluorescent lighting. Living rooms are good, as are office spaces with lots of natural lighting, plants, comfortable seating, etc. If you're planning a large meeting, there are free spaces you can use at libraries, community centres and at City Hall. At your first meeting, try to establish a clear mandate, or position statement, that describes why your group exists. Always end each meeting by summarizing assigned tasks and choosing the date for your next meeting. Don't lose momentum!

Identify and connect with stakeholders and allies

Who else cares about this issue? Talk to other groups in your community and citywide organizations who might have an interest in the topic. Keep detailed lists of who you've spoken to. Can they endorse your campaign? Can they offer any resources like photocopiers or meeting space? Do they have a good relationship with the media or with the local councillor? You don't need to invite these people into your core team, but keep in them in the loop and involved. A good way to do this is to create a separate advisory committee comprised of stakeholders and allied groups.

Make a brand

What's the name of your project or campaign? Short, witty names are good. The 'Clean Train Coalition' is better than 'Coalition of Residents Opposed to Diesel Trains in our Neighbourhood.' Alliteration is always good: 'Better Ballots' is better than 'Improved Ballots.' Catchy acronyms are also good. 'Toronto Environmental Alliance' is clunky, but the acronym, TEA, is great. Make it fun and friendly. The 'Beautiful City Billboard Fee' was originally called the 'Visual Pollution Tax.' By focusing on the positive instead of the negative, the project increased its political viability. The group's final name was 'BeautifulCity.ca.' Short and simple.

Produce materials

Take your brand, your slogan and key messages and create some simple materials you can use to promote your campaign, group or project. Some materials should be information-heavy (with the

data and information from your research) and some should be simple and sexy (like buttons and stickers).

Avoid photocopying, if you can. Colour lends credibility and legitimacy to your project, and colour printing has become affordable.

You'll also want to put up a website at this point, and to start a Facebook group. Don't be intimidated by either. Find someone who is familiar with web design and social media and put them to work! A website can be very simple: it's just a place where people can find basic information about your initiative. It has to look clean and professional, but it doesn't have to be fancy.

Start to gather email addresses

Your project should have an email list. Even in the age of Facebook and Twitter, a well-organized email list is quite powerful. If it's a small campaign, you can make one on your own (in Word or Excel). For bigger projects, you can use online tools like Constant Contact, MailerMailer, Mailchimp, Campaign Monitor and Bronto, which provide a customized sign-up form and allow you to send targeted messages. Collecting email addresses allows you to gradually build a growing list of supporters who will support your campaign by attending events, sending letters and volunteering. Make it simple for people to sign up, and send them a monthly newsletter to tell them what's happening and remind them of how they can get involved.

Organize an event

Once you have a team, materials and some supporters, it's time to go public. Announce a public event, and use all your connections, tools and networks to bring out a crowd. Be bold and book a good-sized space. Give people at least two weeks' notice. You can make it a fun event, with refreshments and music, but don't forget about the politics. Invite a few speakers and set up an information table and a sign-up sheet. This event should be fun *and* informative. Hand out lots of materials and invite everyone to the next event and/or meeting. Each event should grow in size as you build momentum towards your goal. Don't forget to document your event with both photos and video that you can post on your new website!

Fundraise

Some campaigns can be run for next to nothing. Other campaigns will require some money for printing materials, venue rental, transportation, event costs, etc.

Don't be scared to ask people for money. Your supporters can contribute in different ways. Some will have time to spare, some will have creativity, some will have energy and some will have money. There is no shame in fundraising. In fact, by asking for money, you're providing an opportunity for people who support your cause to contribute, which will make them feel good and connected to the campaign.

Use the media

The media is much more accessible than you think. There are editors and writers waiting for local stories to appear so they have content for their  next issue. There is no official or 'proper' format for a press release. Be creative. Send a message to media outlets with a short and concise message. You have to convince them, in one page,

that you have something to say that is important, relevant, cred-
ible, current and interesting (see Jennifer Lewington's essay,
starting on page 190, for more on how to do this). Provide
contact information and keep track of who responds. Be
prepared to do interviews: develop a few clear talking points, and
anticipate the questions and counter-arguments you might
encounter. Invite the media to your events, and don't forget
about the small local newspapers, which are always looking for
community initiatives to highlight. Build relationships with
supportive journalists. They're a valuable resource – work closely
with them.

Gather public and political endorsements

Who supports your campaign? Write a clear paragraph that
summarizes the position or goal of your project and ask people
to endorse it. Start with your strongest supporters and then
build from there. Does anyone on your team know any celebri-
ties? Do any politicians (or former politicians) support your
project? As you get more endorsements, put any high-profile
names and photos on your website, on your flyers and in your
newsletters.

Identify a political champion

If your campaign requires the support of
City Council, you'll want to have one
councillor act as your political champion
at City Hall. Councillors can tell you
what's happening behind the scenes and
can use their resources to get you quick
access to information from staff. They
can book meeting space for you. They can
speak to the media. And they can stand up

at council meetings and speak on your behalf, putting forward your message and arguments.

Use all resources to support political process

Once you've got your champion on the inside, let her advise you on strategy and timeline. Using your website, newsletter, volunteers and events, mobilize all your supporters to put pressure on the political process. Sometimes all you need is twenty letters of support sent to a councillor. For a bigger campaign, you might need 200 people at City Council. Don't give up. There will be bumps and distractions and frustrations. Keep your machine well-oiled and running.

Celebrate!

So, you've done it. Your campaign was successful, and you and your supporters got (mostly) what you wanted. It's time to celebrate! We often forget to applaud our own efforts and to thank those who've helped along the way. We complain loudly when council doesn't do what we want, but we rarely celebrate when they deliver. Celebrations are an opportunity to show gratitude to council, and to thank your community supporters and volunteers. It's a chance to remind everyone how much work went into the campaign, and that change is possible.

Remember that no project is too small or too big. Your party might be a group of a hundred people gathered at a restaurant to celebrate a major new policy at City Hall. Or it could be a handful of people in your kitchen celebrating a new speed bump that makes your street safer for children.

But wait! You're not done. Continue to monitor the situation to ensure that council and staff follow through with their decision.

Next steps

After you've won and had a chance to relax, start back at the top with another idea! Civic engagement doesn't end. It takes breaks, but it's a way of life. It's for those who aren't comfortable sitting back and hoping others will change things for them. It's for people who can see a better community and are willing to work towards it.

While you're fighting for change, keep in mind that good leaders know how to take care of themselves. Make sure to pace yourself, delegate responsibilities and avoid burnout by watching for signs of stress. Take as much free time as you need to find a place of balance and health. Only then can you be a successful leader and agent of change.

Dave Meslin is a Toronto-based artist and organizer who has instigated a variety of urban projects, including Reclaim the Streets, the Toronto Public Space Committee, *Spacing* magazine, City Idol, Human River, Toronto Cyclists Union, the WindFest Kite Festival, *Dandyhorse* magazine and the Ranked Ballot Initiative. When he's not deeply immersed in urban politics or electoral reform, Dave tours with local pop band the Hidden Cameras. Multipartisan and fiercely optimistic, Dave embraces ideas and projects that cut across traditional boundaries between grassroots politics, electoral politics and the arts community.

Marlena Zuber lives and works in Toronto. She makes maps, illustrates books and magazines, produces drawings and paintings and is a member of the glam-pop indie band Tomboyfriend (www.myspace.com/ tomboyfriend). She also assists in running the non-profit art program Creative Works Studio (www.creativeworks-studio.ca). In 2008, Marlena partnered with writer Stacey May Fowles (www.staceymayfowles.com) to produce the illustrated novel *Fear of Fighting*, published by Invisible Publishing (invisiblepublishing.heroku.com). She recently completed a large series of maps and drawings for *Stroll*, a monograph of Toronto from a *flâneur*'s perspective, by Shawn Micallef.

Ramping Up
John Lorinc

In the late 1990s, Nick Pierre and his buddies, all teens with a consuming interest in skateboarding, would regularly gravitate to the grounds of East York Civic Centre, an often deserted plaza with the sort of concrete ramps, benches and curbs that attract skateboarders. They didn't really cause any trouble, but the fact of their presence attracted the centre's security guards, who would brusquely chase them off the grounds. As Pierre recalls, 'We were constantly being kicked out.'

Their crime: ollies, grinds, a bit too much noise. And, of course, their age. But Pierre and his buddies were unusually dedicated boarders. In 1998, they'd created something called Team East York, which involved setting up ramps in schoolyards and holding boarding contests for local teens, complete with prizes and videos. Not surprisingly, they weren't easily deterred by the Civic Centre's security troops, and they kept returning to the East York grounds.

One day, a local city councillor strolled out to talk to Pierre's group, and he had a suggestion: why don't they set up an organization and start a petition asking for a skateboard park? Pierre, then eighteen, took up the challenge. He and his group collected names and presented their petition to the councillor (Pierre doesn't recall his name), who dutifully promised to look for money in the East York parks budget. They'd engaged.

But the moment soon passed. In 1998, amalgamation begat the megacity, and in the ensuing bureaucratic chaos, their nascent proposal for a skate park disappeared, seemingly without a trace. As for Pierre and his pals, they grew older.

When it comes to public space, groups of apparently idle teenagers, especially males, make adults edgy. As a society, we'd

Nick Pierre at Stan Wadlow Skatepark

prefer they disperse and go elsewhere, where we can't see or hear them. And when they don't comply, we press the point by passing anti-loitering bylaws, banning ball hockey from residential streets,[1] bumping up security and even taking physically exclusionary steps, like erecting fences or installing 'skate-stoppers' – small stone or steel knobs designed to prevent boarders (and BMX bikers) from doing tricks on benches, rails and retaining walls.

The design of urban and quasi-private open space attests to the fact that our society subtly but systematically discourages youth from congregating in public. Toronto's parks, for example, are generously equipped with playgrounds for children, dog runs for pet owners, baseball and soccer pitches for amateur sports clubs, lawn-bowling greens, tennis courts, golf courses, municipal rinks, community centres, gardens, trails and public art.

1 Ball-hockey enthusiasts in various parts of Canada have sought to reverse those long-standing bylaws, with the City of Kingston leading the way with a new approach that allows kids to play on residential streets with certain conditions. In Toronto, *Spacing* magazine publisher Matt Blackett has launched a similar push to legalize a sport that once dominated Canadian neighbourhoods.

Yes, teens can use these amenities if they wish, but most are not built with youth in mind. The baseball and tennis clubs charge fees, operate according to schedules and are generally populated by adults. Recreation programming tends to be geared to kids under thirteen. Go to a city indoor pool, and one finds older people doing laps. Teens who decide to goof around on playground equipment are shooed away by parents with younger children. Civic gardens, with their tended flower beds and horticultural variety, have scant appeal.

Toronto's ravines, of course, are great places to ride and hang out, if you happen to live near one, but many neighbourhoods have no such access. What's left? Dreary schoolyards and hundreds of hectares of nondescript lawns, suitable for activities like Frisbee or football, as well as a scattering of volleyball courts, outdoor rinks for pickup hockey (if you're lucky enough to live near one) and of course the ubiquitous basketball courts, with their cracked asphalt and shredded nets.

Some city institutions have tried to reach out. Toronto Community Housing recently decided to cut back on its children's programs and reallocate those resources to youth living in the city's far-flung network of low-income housing projects. The extensive Toronto Public Library system has invested heavily in internet computer terminals and wifi service, and there's less shushing. As well, there are various youth drop-in centres around the city, especially in disadvantaged neighbourhoods where they may be part of a tutoring service. Though they're typically run on shoestring budgets cobbled together from grants and donations, many of these places are now equipped with digital media equipment meant to appeal to kids who want to record music or beats, design websites, conduct job searches or just trawl YouTube (see sidebar).

But all of these places operate well within the constraints of adult supervision, and thus hold limited appeal to youth who

In 1990, the Ontario government and the Centre for Addiction and Mental Health established a small drop-in centre in Regent Park with a mandate to help combat drug use among the poor and ethnically diverse residents of Canada's oldest public housing project. Not long after, the facility hired a youth worker named Adonis Huggins. The son of Caribbean parents who settled in Kensington Market, Huggins spent time in his own youth hanging out at a drop-in centre on Bellevue, and went on to study at George Brown College and then Dalhousie.

Not long after starting, Huggins discovered that the way to get uncommunicative young people to talk about their concerns was to hand them a video camera and let them run with it. 'We discovered that youth can make the lousiest videos, but they'll watch [them] forever, because they can see themselves,' he told the *Globe and Mail* in 2006.

Regent Park Focus Youth Media Arts Centre, as Huggins' shoestring basement operation came to be known, gradually expanded into a wide range of other forms of communication, including a magazine (*Catch Da Flava*), photography, music, graphic arts and new media. The Focus Centre also has its own television and radio station, and the programming is now available via podcasts and on YouTube. All the content is developed and produced by local youth, who can drop in between 11 and 5 p.m.

Besides Huggins, Focus has a handful of staff and supports itself with grants and in-kind donations. Focus graduates, despite growing up in a low-income neighbourhood with chronic crime and drug issues, have found careers in graphic design, video production, journalism, marketing, communications and engineering.

desire less structure and more independence in their lives. Indeed, it's hardly surprising that many teens are far more likely to gravitate to shopping malls or food courts, where they can blend into the crowd.

In the private realm, youth from better-off families may have dedicated spaces in their homes to gather – rec rooms, attic bedrooms and so on – and they may even have alternatives, like cottages, ski lodges, etc. Those who live in more modest circumstances often find themselves relegated to literally marginal spaces, like stairwells, hydro corridors and the dead zones between apartment complexes.

The City's indifference to this segment of society becomes apparent when we explore the significant disconnect between political promises and actual government commitment to the needs of young people.

When Mel Lastman was mayor, Council designated downtown councillor Olivia Chow, now a federal MP, as its child and youth 'advocate.' That appointment led to strategic plans and an 'action committee,' but little by way of concrete results.

Mayor David Miller carried on the rhetorical tradition, establishing a child, youth and education 'round table' that later morphed into a 'youth strategy panel,' chaired by budget chief and ex-school trustee Shelley Carroll. He also enlisted former chief justice Roy McMurtry to develop a community safety plan whose mandate included issues such as youth services and employment in the City's thirteen 'priority neighbourhoods.'

There's certainly a public policy case to be made for such efforts: according to the 2006 census, there are approximately 300,000 youth (ages twelve to twenty-two) in the City of Toronto – accounting for slightly more than a tenth of the total population.

But while City Council has active committees and task forces for all sorts of other constituencies (cyclists, tenants, pedestrians, seniors, etc.), the youth panel petered out quickly, despite an enthusiastic initial response to calls for volunteer panel members. After all, teens, in spite of their numbers, don't vote, don't pay property taxes, mostly don't own cars, often can't afford user fees, have no idea how to hire a lobbyist and like attending evening meetings even less than adults do.

The lack of clout seems particularly evident in the shortage of recreational opportunities for youth. A 2006 consultant's report on a Toronto Parks Renaissance Strategy observed that, compared to children, youth 'are not well served' by the City's recreation facilities. Its advice: let youth develop their own programming and develop facilities like skateboard and BMX parks, especially in low-income areas.

Yet this straightforward advice doesn't filter through to the people who decide how the City should allocate its resources. According to information provided by Parks, Forestry and Recreation officials, the City will spend $16.1 million of its capital budget on new youth-oriented recreation facilities between 2005 and 2019 – a fourteen-year period. Despite the long time horizon, this outlay encompasses just twenty-three projects (as of April 2010), including a few cricket pitches, new volleyball and basketball courts, youth lounges (one will be built in a former rifle range) and a handful of skateboard parks.

Besides those investments, the City, together with various funding partners, expects to spend $33.7 million between 2007 and 2011 in a range of new projects in the thirteen priority neighbourhoods, as per one of former mayor Miller's 2006 election promises. A large chunk of that cash will end up building or expanding community centres and daycare facilities for low-income families. Based on a breakdown of the project spending provided by the City, approximately $12 million of this total will go specifically to youth-related projects (e.g., youth 'lounges,' sports pads, etc.).

In sum, the City of Toronto will have spent $28 million on youth-oriented facilities by the end of this decade. Sounds like a lot? To put the figure into context, consider the following comparisons.

• The straightening of Dufferin Street near Queen West and Gladstone – a solution in search of a problem – has cost the City $40 million.
• The dragon-boat course off Marilyn Bell Park had a $27 million price tag.
• The City budgeted $42.7 million for revitalizing Nathan Phillips Square.
• The proposed Fort York visitors' centre is an $18 million project.
• Between 2010 and 2019, the City plans to invest $35 million to beautify business improvement area streetscapes (i.e., planters, public art, etc.).
• Roads, bridges, sidewalks, potholes and other transportation infrastructure will gobble up a hefty $2.2 billion between 2010 and 2019. That's eighty times more than the cumulative expenditure on youth-specific facilities between 2005 and 2019.

Here's one more: the restoration of Edwards Gardens and the Toronto Civic Garden Centre, completed in the early 2000s, came in at $6 million. Donations covered most of the budget (there are lots of corporate sponsors in the gardening world, after all), while the City contributed $600,000. But fundraising also plays a crucial role in lower-profile public-space enhancements. Neighbourhood groups, especially in affluent areas, not only advocate for improved local parks; homeowners often band together to raise tens of thousands of dollars for playgrounds, which make those communities kid-friendly and drive up property values. In theory, savvy and sympathetic adults could persuade skateboard equipment manufacturers to help finance new skate parks for local youth. But when was the last time you heard about homeowners and local businesses actually getting together to fundraise for a public-space improvement specifically for teens?

In 2003, five years after Nick Pierre's short-lived attempt to lobby for a skateboard park, he got an unexpected call from a City of Toronto parks official, who wanted to know if there was still interest among East York teens in a skate park. The bureaucrat told Pierre he had about $60,000 to spend on temporary ramps and wanted to find a suitable location. At the time, there was just one permanent, purpose-built skate park in the city (at Leslie and Cummer in North York, built at the urging of the local councillor David Shiner) and a few more temporary ones under development. The City eventually chose Greenwood Park – a large, flat green space in the east end with three baseball diamonds and a pool – where it installed a handful of wooden and metal ramps on a concrete tennis court pad. 'The ramps,' sniffs Pierre, who is now an employment counsellor, 'were poorly designed, made from bad materials. And there was no input from the community' – by which he means skateboarders – 'as to what they wanted. It was, "Here you are."'

Skateboarding is hardly a new pastime, but it has experienced something of a renaissance in the past fifteen years or so with the rise of snowboarding and the associated fashion/equipment trends. Stripped down, this activity is well-suited to kids of a certain age: skateboarding entails a measure of physical risk and a very adolescent sort of dexterity. There are tricks to be practiced obsessively. There's jargon, all the nerdy technical detail about the gear and the urban grunge appeal. And, of course, it does not involve adult supervision or any sort of scheduling.

As a fairly affordable outdoor activity, in fact, there's much to recommend skateboarding, and yet Toronto has neglected its potential to engage, largely because of the lingering misperception among adults that skateboarding is linked to drugs, violence, noise and garbage.

By contrast, many other North American cities get the skateboard story, but none quite so thoroughly as Vancouver, whose original skatepark, China Creek, marked its thirtieth anniversary in 2010. Today, there are almost fifty permanent skateboard parks across Greater Vancouver, and communities clamour for more.

It was not always the case. In the late 1990s – a period of turmoil in Vancouver due to the spike of overdose deaths in the Downtown Eastside – the municipality began clamping down on skateboarders who congregated on the open plazas of the business district. The City passed strict anti-boarding ordinances and then gave police the authority to seize skateboards. 'It was illegal to skate anywhere,' recalls Vancouver Park Board commissioner Sarah Blyth, a thirty-seven-year-old social worker. (VPB commissioners are elected.) 'Where were all these people to go?' It was a question some youth posed to police when they received a ticket, and of course the officers didn't have a good answer.

Long before she was elected to the VPB, Blyth loved skateboarding. Recognizing the lack of venues, she and a friend set up an indoor skate park for boarders willing to pay an entrance fee. They rented an old warehouse at the end of False Creek and filled it with ramps and pool tables, but the business folded after just eighteen months.

Undaunted, Blyth made a cold call to the VPB to ask if the City was willing to build skateboarding facilities. She was referred to a civil servant named Mark Vulliamy, who managed the community centre where that original China Creek skate park was located. As a recreation manager, Vulliamy recognized that the VPB understood how to cater to the needs of children, adults and seniors. 'But really not much has been built for teens except basketball courts,' he observes.

As a city bureaucrat, Vulliamy also knew that many cities, including Vancouver, had soured on skate parks out of a fear of liability exposure arising from injuries incurred on municipal property. 'It sent a chill through civic administrations everywhere,' he says. At China Creek, VPB officials decided to avoid the risk by asking users to sign waivers releasing the City from liability. Those waivers provided more than just legal cover; when Vulliamy and his staff analyzed the forms, they saw the park was attracting kids from across Vancouver.

Vulliamy, like Blyth, had mounting concerns about how the City was 'locking down' public space. So he offered her some insider advice: she and her friends, he said, should set up an association, figure out what they wanted and petition the board for more skate parks. And so in 1999, the Vancouver Skateboarding Coalition, now a political force in the city, was born.

Blyth's nascent group soon found itself working with the Parks Board on a proposed venue for new skateboard parks. They zeroed in on several locations, ultimately selecting a piece of fallow City property between a viaduct and the future site of the Olympic Village. But their efforts met with a wall of strident opposition during public consultations with irate homeowners. 'People were pretty honest about not wanting youth in their neighbourhoods,' recounts Blyth. In the post-Expo years, Vancouver had built superb parks, trails and boardwalks for cyclists, runners, pedestrians and inline skaters. Skateboarders, however, weren't welcome.

Yet Blyth didn't give up. The coalition organized numerous public skateboard skills demonstrations and helmet safety sessions designed to dispel the tenacious stereotypes. She also encouraged her members to round up endorsements from relatives and other adults. 'We got letters from senior citizens who

said they'd been afraid but discovered [skateboarding] was cool,'
says Blyth.

Vulliamy, in turn, paid close attention to the feedback. At one
point, the VPB distributed a questionnaire in one of the new
condos on False Creek, asking residents for their views on the
proposed facility. When he read through the responses, he
noticed that some had messages alerting City officials to the fact
that a small group of naysayers had staked out the ballot boxes
and were urging residents to oppose the proposal. As it tran-
spired, however, 70 per cent of the thousand questionnaires
collected approved. 'The vocal opposition wasn't reflective of the
community's attitudes,' Vulliamy says.

In the end, the VPB built the new skate park, and would go
on to develop many more throughout the 2000s. Vancouver
council, in turn, approved relaxed skateboard regulations in
2003 to allow skaters to use the roads – a widely supported
move in a city that played host to one of North America's largest
skateboard jams.[2] Blyth credits these victories to a combination
of political savvy, determined public education campaigns, focus
and patience. Vulliamy observes that politicians in Greater
Vancouver no longer make hay by opposing skate parks because
they understand that the users of such recreational amenities
don't actually fit that outdated stereotype. 'The lesson,' he coun-
sels, 'is learn to mobilize, learn to lobby and learn to advocate.'

In 2005, back in Toronto, Nick Pierre's request for a permanent
skate park landed on the desk of Janet Davis, a left-leaning East
York city councillor. She tracked him down and asked if he'd work
with parks staff to develop a plan. Pierre, by then, was twenty-five,
but still an avid boarder. Davis, an ally of former mayor David

2 Jane Armstrong: 'He's no poser, dude: City planner Michael Gordon had a personal
reason for wanting Vancouver's skateboarding rules relaxed this month – he rides 22
blocks to work each day.' *Globe and Mail*, May 17, 2003.

Miller, told him she had about $300,000 to spend. After conferring with City officials, 'it quickly became apparent they didn't know what to build, how much it would cost, what it would look like,' Pierre recalls. 'They had no idea who would be using it.'

The City wanted the new facility built in Stan Wadlow Park, a large and frequently unused open space in a working-class area near Woodbine and O'Connor that had several baseball diamonds, a rink, a clubhouse, a playground and a rockery. Wadlow is bounded on two sides by private homes and a seniors' residence. The skate park was to be built next to the garden.

Davis rounded up a steering committee with representatives of the baseball clubs, the neighbourhood and the East York Garden Club, which had maintained that rockery for decades. Malcolm Geast, the past president of the club and a retired Environment Canada employee, told me he initially balked at the idea: a busy skate park would undermine the tranquility of the rockery. The baseball clubs, in turn, complained vigorously to Davis that they'd lose some of 'their' outfield. Then, during public meetings, a handful of the homeowners facing the park objected vociferously to the plan, warning ominously of noise, drugs and 'unwelcome elements.' The irony, Pierre says, is that Stan Wadlow already had a bit of a problem with kids who'd congregate behind the bushes at night, drinking and sniffing model-airplane glue.

In some ways, the process played out in much the same way as had happened in Vancouver. As a counterpoint to the sometimes 'hysterical' objections of a few homeowners, Pierre and his friends took care to be cordial and constructive at the meetings, working to educate the community about the nature of skateboarding. They brought along parents and grandparents to speak in support of their pastime. And, to counter fears, he pointed out that drinking wouldn't be a problem because it's too hard to board when intoxicated. They also pledged to make sure the users would help keep the facility free of litter. As he noted, it's risky to skate on surfaces strewn with broken glass.

During the design process, which dragged on for much of 2006, Geast proposed straightforward noise-mitigation measures, such as a sufficient setback from nearby homes (42 metres), as well as a berm to buffer the skate park from the rockery. 'Our perception of what noise there would be was misplaced,' he recalls.

Pierre, meanwhile, turned his attention to the layout of the park itself. His group, about fifteen friends from fourteen to thirty years in age, fanned out to east-end 'street spots' to encourage youth to come to a one-day design workshop with city planners and landscape architects. There are all sorts of skate park features possible – bowls, ramps, rails, benches, walls, plazas, graffiti murals, etc. – and he wanted the ultimate design to reflect local tastes. About fifty youth turned out. But Pierre also understood his group had to closely monitor the approvals process to prevent bureaucratic mistakes, such as excessive restrictions or the construction of a fence around the site that would 'totally ruin the vibe,' as he says. 'There has to be that element of freedom.'

Finally, in early 2007, after a year of planning and almost a decade after Pierre's initial exchange with that East York city councillor, the Stan Wadlow Skatepark opened, making it the third permanent skate park in Canada's largest city (another facility, the Vanderhoof/Leonard Linton Skatepark, had opened in 2005 in a park near Eglinton and Laird). There are a few others under development, including a mammoth $1.7 million facility, opened in the fall of 2009, on some parkland near Ashbridges Bay and the boardwalk in the Beach. Another is slated for southern Etobicoke, in a park near Islington and Lakeshore; construction of the $600,000 project – financed with City cash, development charges and donations from a concrete company – began in the fall of 2010, after several years of controversy. As of late 2010, no others are planned. The City, for the record, has set up a handful of temporary skate parks in outdoor skating rinks, equipped with clanging metal or wooden ramps. But these tend to disappear quickly whenever local residents raise a fuss ... about the noise.

Skateboarding isn't the only vaguely transgressive, youth-oriented activity to encounter push-back from planners and teen-averse homeowners. Take BMX biking, which, for many adults, is still linked to caricatures of overgrown males tearing around on what appear to be souped-up kids' bikes. Some assume those bikes are stolen from children and used to ferry drugs ...

In fact, BMX biking began in the 1970s, on the original dirt bikes, and became a fixture of the extreme sport circuit over the past decade or so, featuring all sorts of aerial stunts and freestyle racing. It enjoyed an Olympics debut during the 2008 summer games in Beijing. But the City of Toronto, for all its rhetoric about the need for more cycling 'infrastructure,' has ignored an exhilarating, free-form, skills-based sport that clearly appeals to youth.

Just weeks before the East York skate park opened, a local BMX enthusiast named Michael Heaton decided to change the dynamic. His plan was to establish a temporary BMX park, made from his own collection of plywood ramps but available to any kids who wanted to test their skills. But he didn't want to jump over all the bureaucratic hurdles that have tripped up so many other Torontonians with ideas and energy. Easier to beg forgiveness, he figured, than to ask permission.

Heaton is an unlikely local hero. A retired teacher at an elite private boys' school, he is a slight man with unruly reddish hair and an elfin manner. Heaton is sixty, but has the physique of a twenty-year-old, tends to dress in baggy slacker clothes and travels everywhere on his BMX bike.

As a teacher, he'd coached whitewater kayaking and was intrigued by the fact that this sport, with its speed and risk, appealed to non-jock kids who didn't fit into more traditional high school teams. When Heaton discovered BMXing at an outdoor education school some years later, it struck him the two sports had much in common, and he became a devotee.

In the late 1990s, Heaton – who runs the popular annual Toronto BMX Jam at the CNE – worked for a time with the City on efforts to find locations for BMX parks. A dirt-bike track did get built near Bayview and Finch, but City officials couldn't settle on other venues. In 2005, they were poised to build a BMX racing track in Marilyn Bell Park, near Ontario Place, but Parkdale residents objected and the plan never got off the ground. That one existing track at Bayview and Finch, for its part, is neglected and difficult to find.

BMX facilities aren't at all like skateboard parks, and the two types of users tend not to mix well; 'tribal competition' is how Wade Nelson, a rider who wrote a PhD thesis on BMX culture, describes the friction. Permanent skate parks are made from smooth concrete, whereas BMX facilities sport several-metre-high plywood ramps, 'street features' (e.g., benches, railings), platforms or dirt trails with jumps. BMX pegs – those aluminum cylinders sticking out of the axles – are used for tricks, but can easily tear up concrete, leaving risky gouges in skate parks.

Nelson points out that Toronto's top BMXers tend to be 'street riders' because there are so few public venues in which to compete and practice; there are two fee-based private indoor BMX parks, but they're far from downtown, in suburban Etobicoke and Markham.

Heaton came up with a quick-and-dirty solution to the impasse. In 2005, he and an entrepreneurial parks official named Allan Crawford built a BMX off-road track – a tight circuit path with jumps, banks and other obstacles – in a neglected and unsafe corner of the Wallace Emerson Community Centre grounds, near Dupont and Dufferin. Heaton found several truckloads of clean fill, Crawford located a City bulldozer and they finished the job in a week, all without the explicit approval of the parks department. 'There was always the threat of it being levelled,' says Heaton.

Two years later, they decided to expand the Wallace Emerson experiment. As the organizer of Toronto BMX Jam, Heaton owns about $50,000 worth of ramps and platforms. Typically, he keeps them in storage, but he started wondering about making them available in a public space. So after the March 2007 Jam wrapped, Heaton rented several tractor trailers and hauled the ramps up to Wallace Emerson, where he and a handful of his BMX circle set them up on a slab of unused concrete that's used as a skating rink in the winter. To ward off lawsuits, they erected a sign warning riders to use the equipment at their own risk.

Over the next three summers, Heaton's graffiti-covered plywood ramps became a major draw for kids living in that part of the west end. (The ramps go into storage in the winters.) The ad-hoc facility attracted about 4,000 youth, many of whom live in the gritty Dufferin-Dupont area. With a bit of funding from the City, Heaton hired some older teens with strong BMX skills to offer lessons to another 400 youth, and he also provided a few dozen bikes for those who didn't have their own equipment. 'That's quite a lot of kids at basically no cost,' he says.

The experiment has had its pitfalls. The dirt course quickly deteriorated and drew anxious inquiries from nearby residents, who fretted that it was becoming an eyesore and a magnet for troublemakers. (The track has been upgraded.) The ramps, in turn, were partially destroyed in a fire in 2008 (Crime Stoppers paid to help rebuild them), but have deteriorated due to use and exposure to the elements. Indeed, academic Wade Nelson points out that, in the summer of 2009, there were injuries because the plywood had begun to rot. It has fallen to Heaton, a private citizen, to finance the repairs and other expenses.

But as the ramps became a warm-weather fixture of the Wallace Emerson community centre, word of the facility and its success has spread rapidly to other corners of the city. For the summer of 2009, Heaton and Const. Scott Mills persuaded Toronto Community Housing officials to set up a temporary BMX park in the parking lot of the Tandridge apartments, a low-income housing complex near Weston Road and Highway 401 that had experienced problems with youth crime. Mills, who runs the Toronto Police Service's 'legal graffiti' program, contributed materials and organizational support so local youth could paint the ramps. An energetic and engaging plainclothes cop who oversees the TPS's Crime Stoppers presence on the internet, Facebook and Twitter, he's worked relentlessly in recent years to promote BMXing to Toronto youth.

To get the program going, TCH hired Jason Tojeiro, who had been one of Heaton's BMX crew at Wallace Emerson, and gave him a $4,000 budget to build some ramps and buy some spare bikes. Mills provided paint and some funding for local kids to cover the ramps with legal graffiti. And TCH also hired Tojeiro and another youth to run the temporary BMX park and provide lessons to the local kids.

'I was a little sceptical at first,' Tojeiro explains one day as he shows off the assortment of wooden ramps he built with his father, a contractor. Growing up in the rough Oakwood/ Vaughan Road area (the so-called Five Points), Tojeiro, now twenty, says he'd been heading down 'a bad road' in his mid-teens. But after attending Heaton's BMX jam at the CNE in 2005, he became intrigued by the sport. He started learning the tricks and ended up spending a lot of time on the Wallace Emerson ramps. 'BMX was a whole new world,' says Tojeiro. 'Addictive, but in a good way.'

Like Tojeiro, many of the local youth were equally dubious about the ramps at Tandridge, but it quickly became apparent that there was a need for them. Kids in the complex had nothing to do in the summer except play video games or shoot hoops. 'You could tell they were heading into a bad place,' he says.

Gradually, curiosity overshadowed animosity, and Tojeiro ended up providing a summer's worth of BMX skills training to about forty local youths, many of whom are now as hooked on this extreme sport as he is. TCH officials told him the Tandridge BMX park was the agency's most successful youth program for the summer of 2009. 'A lot of the participants,' Tojeiro remarks, 'their lives have changed.' Why? Because you can't do BMX tricks when you're stoned. 'You get really busy and involved with the sport so there's no time to get involved with the bad stuff.'

These ultra-low-budget successes have not been lost on City officials. In October 2009, Janet Davis, who chaired the community development and recreation committee, spearheaded a push to get Council's approval for a 'BMX Go Forward Strategy' that laid out a plan to address the enormous mismatch between the demand for off-road or BMX biking facilities (the number of riders was estimated to be about 100,000) and the city's two lonely facilities, one of which exists only because of Michael Heaton's generosity.

The new strategy identifies a wide range of potential venues – the handful of existing skateboard parks, park trails, school parking lots, ski hills, surplus municipal buildings, hydro corridors, community centres, etc. But, apart from a promise to spend $200,000 to repair the Wallace Emerson ramps, the plan didn't propose a budget, nor a solution to the problem of overcoming the insistent NIMBYism that can easily undermine these kinds of projects.

Tellingly, City staff took care to point out in their report that such a plan has a range of ancillary benefits, including improving tourism, supporting the extreme sport industries and keeping up with rural areas in Southern Ontario that aggressively promote off-road biking. Providing Toronto youth with more recreational choices is evidently not sufficient justification.

Janet Davis argues that skate and BMX parks offer a double-barrelled benefit: they provide youth with challenging and novel physical activities. And, she points out, such projects can give local youth – the Nick Pierres and Jason Tojeiros of this city – an opportunity to become actively involved in the design and operation of the facility. 'They're the ones who know best what works,' she asserts. 'They have a real sense of ownership for the facility when it's done. You've got to believe their involvement will make a difference.'

For Nick Pierre and his friends on Team East York, it's not just an article of faith. They've taken it upon themselves to keep the skate park relatively clean, and they chased off a group of kids who used to sit in that corner of the park and drink. The fifty-odd youth who participated in the original design consultation exercise and the painting of the graffiti murals now protect the facility as if it belonged to them. And some of those angry homeowners near the park have admitted to Pierre, who skates there most days after work, that their fears were unfounded. Malcolm Geast confirms the point: 'I haven't heard any complaints since the park has gone in.'

Today, Stan Wadlow Park is livelier and better used year round than it was ever before. The gangs, noise and drugs turned out to be a phantom menace.

The lessons are not difficult to fathom: in Toronto, it takes organization, well-connected politicians and superhuman patience to persuade the City to build fairly basic amenities for youth. But each such undertaking is vulnerable to the familiar litany of objections from residents who'd just as soon not have to live near venues that attract teens. Equally problematic is the

Nick Pierre

City's chronic internal disorganization, as projects are delayed interminably due to vagaries about funding.

What's also clear is the City's lack of imagination – which Michael Heaton attributes to an aging Parks and Recreation bureaucracy – militates against the embrace of new forms of recreation and new approaches to engaging young people.

Consider that in the last fifteen years or so, hundreds of local recreation entrepreneurs have moved to fill the breach, launching venues in vacant industrial spaces that offer everything from trampolines to indoor rock-climbing, fencing, beach volleyball, roller hockey and, most recently, 'parkour' clubs (indoor climbing/obstacle course facilities). But these are all for-profit operations that charge commercial fees, and therefore exclude those who can't afford to play.

Is there any reason why the City couldn't use part of its annual recreation programming budget to purchase time in these facilities and make the slots available to youth and kids from low-income families? Or, alternatively, why can't Parks and Recreation negotiate joint ventures with these entrepreneurs to develop satellite operations on City-owned land? Unable to envision new ways of conducting its core business, the City takes the path of least resistance with its youth programs: midnight basketball, some drop-in centres and not much else.

It's worth emphasizing that almost all youth endure this brand of societal indifference. Yet kids from more affluent backgrounds tend to have many more recreational options available to them, many of which are fee-based and delivered in private settings (overnight camps, ski resorts, sports leagues, musical equipment rentals, drama/arts programs, etc.). For young people growing up in modest or low-income homes, there are far fewer diversions, and thus greater risk.

Indeed, there is considerable perversity in the City's demonstrable reluctance to act. The harder we work to keep young people out of our parks and public spaces because we don't like their noise or their gear, the more we push them towards genuine trouble. After all, teenage boredom is a potent source of negative energy that can be highly combustible when mixed with poverty, drugs and gangs.

On that point, the Ontario government in 2008 commissioned former speaker Alvin Curling and retired chief justice Roy McMurtry to oversee a high-level assessment of the 'roots of youth violence' in the wake of the shooting death of fifteen-year-old Jordan Manners inside C. W. Jeffreys Collegiate, in North York.[3]

Their report identifies a range of 'roots' including poverty, racism and undiagnosed mental health problems. But it also noted the 'dearth' of recreational and arts facilities and 'community hubs' in high-needs urban neighbourhoods. As the authors put it, 'Well-resourced and readily accessible arts and

3 *The Review of the Roots of Youth Violence*, by Hon. Roy McMurtry and Dr. Alvin Curling, Executive Summary, p. 20. www.children.gov.on.ca/htdocs/ English/documents/topics/youthandthelaw/rootsofyouthviolence-vol2.pdf.

recreation facilities should be available on a reliable, sustained basis, and youth should be involved in designing the programs to be offered in those facilities.'

Nick Pierre didn't need a $2 million expert study to figure out that last bit. Thanks to his group's perseverance, Toronto's public spaces are just a little more welcoming to a broad range of youth in a mixed-income East York neighbourhood. In turn, the young people who brought the Stan Wadlow Skatepark to life and now attend to its upkeep have emerged as more fully engaged members of their community – not just a gang of layabouts with an irritating pastime. Along the way, they learned some important lessons about getting things done, building consensus within a diverse community and representing their own interests to officialdom – all experiences that will serve them well throughout their lives.

But as Pierre and his friends would be the first to say, this project was never an eat-your-veggies exercise in civic education. It was always about, well, grinding out a great place to skate in our own concrete jungle. The rest, as they say, is icing.

Get involved

catchdaflava.com   torontobmx.ca

eyskate.com   wallaceemerson.ca

John Lorinc is a Toronto-based journalist. Author of *The New City* (Penguin, 2006), he writes regularly about urban affairs for the *Globe and Mail* and *Spacing*, and has contributed essays to each of the previous volumes of the *uTOpia* series (Coach House). He bought a skateboard in Grade 7 for $10, but never mastered using it.

Denise Balkissoon

About face

Moving towards a City that looks like the city

It's a clash of clichés: the public face of Toronto versus the Public Face of Toronto.

The former is found in Yonge-Dundas Square during an Olympic hockey game, say, or any weekday morning on the TTC. Moms feed their kids samosas and proffer drinking boxes of soy milk. Teenagers chatter in Amharic and Spanish, their facial features very different, their skinny jeans exactly the same.

Then move to the Council chambers at City Hall or the Legislative Assembly at Queen's Park. There are a few olive- or brown-skinned faces, a smattering of proper business skirts and sensible pumps and then, uniformly, a sea of white men: 69 of 107 MPPs and 25 of 44 city councillors, if you're counting.

In a city that's predicted to be 67 per cent non-white by 2031, let's assume this snapshot is problematic. Let's take for granted that democracy is frustrated when stubborn issues of income, language and prejudice prevent certain groups of people from becoming prime minister. Consider it a given that electoral politics is the ultimate form of civic engagement because elected bodies set policy that affects energy, schools, passports, pools and, of course, taxes. If renters don't vote and refugees aren't allowed to cast a ballot, their issues won't get much play in the hallowed halls of government. Agreed.

What's up for debate is whether a lack of engagement with Public Life really means a lack of engagement with public life.

A few years ago, I interviewed a young Jamaican-Canadian man and we shared some laughs about life with immigrant parents. But then we got to discussing our parents' resistance to non-traditional immigrant careers (i.e., something other than engineer or doctor).

He scoffed that I might have the same problems as him, since my dad, Bas Balkissoon, is a public figure – an MPP who was a city councillor for many years. He's not totally right, but I see his point. I know that, mispronounced or not, Balkissoon is a name that's on the public radar, and that in certain ways the path into public life has been less rocky for me than for others.[1]

As far as I know, my dad is the city's first South Asian–Trinidadian councillor and now MPP, even though the 2006 census says 4.2 per cent of the city is Caribbean. He represents a suburban riding that's very far from the downtown centre of power. When he first ran, in the late '80s, elected representatives didn't even send out newsletters to northeast Scarborough. Habitually disappointed residents were wary of his overtures at first, but that changed over the years, and community meetings that used to attract only a handful of citizens now see forty or fifty participants. To politics junkies, he's known for fiscal prudence, especially with regard to the MFP computer scandal.[2] In Scarborough–Rouge River, he's the one behind two decades' worth of community centres and libraries and, this year, a long-awaited health clinic that serves clients in nine languages. When asked about the journey from subsidized housing at Jane and Finch to this, he shrugs. 'A lot of immigrants wouldn't think about trying for the type of work I got into,' is all he'll say. We often disagree on politics, journalism and where to have dinner, but my dad is someone that I (and a lot of other non-white suburbanites, judging from the number of people who name-check him) can point to as a representative of a different Toronto than the one on magazine

1 It's kind of cool that both *Toronto Life* and the *Toronto Star* have used the word 'brown' in their coverage in the past year. Casual recognition means you're in.
2 In 2001, he was the chair of the City's Audit Committee when it brought to light a dubious computer leasing deal between the City and MFP Financial. A public inquiry eventually confirmed that corruption, bribery and improperly tendered contracts cost taxpayers at least $80 million.

covers. Yet I still find that the minefield of identity can be a real turnoff to an attempt to enter public life.

First, there's the betrayal problem, where people who share a part of your identity don't like what you've said or done. Here, detractors think they can somehow decree you're no longer a Jew or a lesbian because of a lockdown on 'airing dirty laundry' in public. This makes it consistently hard to find interview subjects, which then invites a slew of criticisms of how non-diverse the media is. There's the tokenism problem, where one Chinese person is made to speak for the thousands of Asians in Toronto. It also means deciding, again and again, whether or not to tell the well-meaning others in the room that just because they're from opposite sides of the Don Valley doesn't mean they remotely represent the whole city. There's the ghettoization problem, balanced with the representation problem: not wanting to be boxed in as the person who deals with suburban issues, yet really caring about suburban public schools and wanting them to get more attention at the same time. Facing all of this, it becomes tempting just to slip into a cubicle and then yell at the television news. I feel like this pretty regularly and I was born here, and my dad's already ensured that 'Balkissoon' gets decent Google hits.

Looking at the top – elected office – the diversity situation is pretty dismal. Yet on the ground, it's awesome. There are so many Torontonians doing so many things to make their communities and their city better. Let's look at those people and celebrate their accomplishments. Then let's talk about how to push them to the top.

Ethnic = voting bloc. And then it doesn't.
Our 2010 mayoral race was cluttered with Italians. Spanning the political spectrum, Italian-Canadian candidates vying for the city's top job brought to the table years of elected and behind-the-scenes political experience. Across the country, there are

Italian city councillors and MPPs, not to mention federal MPs and a senator. When pundits decry the dearth of immigrants in Canadian politics, they surely don't mean Italians.

In today's Toronto, Italians are kind of white, but that wasn't always the case. Those who came before World War II were Catholics who had moved to a Protestant town and who were ridiculed for their purported big noses and hairiness. Facing discriminatory 1920s immigration policies, it was often hard for them to find jobs and, on occasion, small Italian businesses were actually burnt down. Many decided to anglicize their names. 'If it was loyalty to your country or your family,' says Angelo Persichilli, political editor of the daily *Corriere Canadese*, 'you chose your family and forgot your heritage.'

The second wave of Italians came to Toronto after the war ended. Our patio culture is thanks entirely to these postwar Italians, who were given loitering tickets for indulging in their continental pastime of convening in the street after dinner to loudly debate their two passions, soccer and politics. But barriers from back home prevented these new Torontonians from getting fully involved.

Before 1960, Toronto's Italians spoke countless different dialects; they couldn't all speak to each other, let alone form a serious political force. Fifty years later, learning English is still the first thing newcomers need to do to pay their bills, never mind making a deposition at City Hall. Attending engineer-specific ESL classes and then sponsoring your brother and moving him into your basement is community involvement on a basic level. It benefits the city at large, helping immigrants to become meaningfully employed, allowing their children to get the most out of their schooling, allowing us to all speak to each other.

Mussolini's legacy also served as a deterrent to mid-century Italian transplants making political noise. 'There was that old love of politics, but also a major mistrust towards institutions,' says Corrado Paina, executive director of the Italian Chamber of Commerce. What happened in the old country will always affect how people act politically in their adopted land. That's relevant today: when wondering why immigrants don't show up to the polls, perhaps consider those whose last election experience involved armed guards. In the summer of 2009, thousands of Tamils lined University Avenue, protesting a war happening half a world away. When their protest marched up the onramp to the Gardiner Expressway, opinions differed as to whether what was happening in Sri Lanka was relevant to Torontonians at large. Some saw the Tamils' actions as civil disobedience, while others felt it was think-global act-local engagement.

In 1960, Joseph J. Piccininni, representing Corso Italia, became the first Italian on Toronto City Council. He had been preceded by an MP, Hamilton's Quinto Martini, and was followed by Charles Caccia, who became MP for Davenport in 1968 and eventually led the federal environment ministry. By the 1980s, Italians in Ontario were significant business owners, had a serious media presence (think CHIN radio) and were a sizeable enough voting bloc to be courted by Bill Davis's Liberals. In 1985, an Italian woman, Betty Disero, won Piccininni's seat in a surprise municipal overthrow, ushering in the modern era for Italian-Torontonians, when it's no longer unthinkable that one member of the community might run against another, or that different Italian politicians might represent very different political viewpoints. In the 2010 mayoral race, there were Italins on the left, on the right and on the fringe. And plenty of Italian-Torontonians ignored that entirely and voted for the person they thought would do the best job.

Smart people doing meaningful things

The summer of 2005, otherwise known as the Summer of the Gun, highlighted the lack of role models for young black men in this city. That's a problem with deep roots, but there are black men in some pretty face-forward positions in Toronto right now. There's Jamaican-born deputy police chief Peter Sloly, controversial school-board director of education Chris Spence, CBC radio host Matt Galloway (who worked his way up from the free weeklies) and David Mitchell, the first chair of Toronto Community Housing to have actually grown up in one of the City's projects.

Mitchell is forty-three years old and spent his adolescence in Lawrence Heights with his mother and four brothers. After high school, he worked in the City's recreation centres, the first place he helped people learn how to advocate for themselves. Choosing what sports programs take place at the local rec centre might not seem like a big deal, but for Mitchell, it's a primer in confidence and negotiation techniques for social-housing parents. 'You can use those skills to meet with somebody in charge when your son gets kicked out of school,' he says.

Mitchell became a jail guard, advancing through the correctional field to become the full-time superintendent of Mimico Correctional Centre. Along the way, he co-founded the Association of Black Law Enforcers, an advocacy group of police officers, prison workers and customs and immigration officials. When he lived in Lawrence Heights in the 1980s, relationships between housing residents and police officers were historically awful. Today, ABLE has given out over $100,000 in scholarships, and David Mitchell is overseeing the transformation of his childhood home into a neighbourhood with opportunities for employment, accessibility and beauty.

Me and my girls

It's cute to hear a grade-schooler switch back and forth between languages, but straddling the divide between two cultures is a pretty big job for a child. 'We grew up pretty fast,' says Huwaida

Osman, who moved to Scarborough from Somalia when she was five. She and her eight siblings were unofficial translators for their parents, mediating meetings with teachers and government officials back when she 'knew English, but at a Grade 3 level.' Despite these adult responsibilities, her parents resisted Osman's own attempts to integrate, suspiciously nixing new ideas like camping.

Osman, now twenty-five, watched as Somali women left high school to take low-paying call-centre jobs, or to get married and simply disappear. In 2007, she and six of her friends decided to start a club for Somali girls and women. The idea was to play pickup basketball and hold some discussion groups, but things have grown much bigger than that. Using a $22,000 federal grant, the group learned about budgets and project managing, building a solid foundation for a long-term organization. They called it Gashanti Unity – the first word means 'young women' in Somali, the second is from a favourite Queen Latifah song. Along with basketball there are tea talks, where girls from across the city spend hours in lively conversation. Soon comes photo and video training to record events for posterity; many Somali events are single-sex, and women tend to have fewer AV skills. After that? In early 2010, Gashanti Unity and the Bay Mills Youth Council landed a $1.8 million grant to build a permanent youth centre in west Scarborough.

A voting bloc on the verge

Another immigrant group that bears looking at is the GTA's Sikhs.[3] Immigrants from the Indian region of Punjab have been coming to Canada for over a century, but older communities largely settled on the west coast (where they, too, met intense prejudice, including being denied the vote until 1948). Most of the GTA's Sikhs were part of two big waves: those who came during the late

3 For most of this history, I thank *Toronto Star* reporter San Grewal.

'60s and early '70s, after the separation of India and Pakistan, and another group that fled sectarian violence in the 1980s.

The question of how political experience back home affects life in a new place is very relevant to Sikhs. In India, the Sikhs are a small but vocal religious minority. Post-partition, Sikhs developed a 'grassroots activist streak,' says the *Star*'s San Grewal, and that level of intense engagement has come with them to the GTA. For Sikhs, city politics is seen as small potatoes – party politics is where it's at, and in the GTA's west end, they're definitely a voting bloc. Despite Ontario's paltry number of non-white MPPS, Sikhs currently hold four of the seven provincial seats in Brampton and Mississauga. There are also a growing number of Sikh MPs nationally. As has happened in the Italian community, Sikh candidates are now running against each other, another sign that their foothold is secure.

Like almost every immigrant group through the last century of Canadian history, save the British,[4] Sikhs have historically been staunch Liberals. Early Sikh supporters threw massive fundraisers and parties, with wealthier members of the community not only footing the bill for space and refreshments, but often the membership fee for those who wanted to carry the Liberal card, says Grewal. Trudeaumania won the red party a solid twenty-five years of newcomer goodwill, but now the Liberals are watching, confused, as the Sikh rock of support very publicly crumbles. It's surprising that the party is surprised: this happened with the Italians, too.

When immigrants become Canadians, they don't vote based solely on ethnicity anymore. Though immigration laws and foreign policy will always be important to them, when newcom-

4 *Beyond the Liberal Party: Immigrant Voting Behaviour in Canada.* Jiyoon Kim, Université de Montréal, and Andrea M. L. Perrella, Wilfrid Laurier University. Prepared for the Annual Meeting of the Canadian Political Science Association, Vancouver, B.C. June 4–7, 2008.

ers are no longer new, they're no longer just Italian, or Sikh, or Chinese, or West Indian. They're also small business owners and mothers and students, casting their ballots after considering all their many interests. The diversifying of political party support is one signal that an ethnic group is Canadian.

Consider that Sikh politicians now range from MPs Ujjal Dosanjh and Ruby Dhalla to Mississauga Centre MPP Harinder Takhar and take another look at the diverse cast of Italian mayoral candidates. It took a decade or three, but these two immigrant groups, at least, are embracing the entire complicated mess of official Canadian politics.

More people redefining 'mainstream'

Alejandra Bravo's main gig is as a manager of the Maytree Foundation, a charity that identifies and nurtures leaders in marginalized communities. But Bravo is involved with a very long list of Toronto organizations, both big and small. She's a citizen member of the Toronto Board of Health and chair of the community engagement program Art Starts. Not least is her work at the schools of her three children, which she says is what gives her 'a sense of place.'

Born in Chile, Bravo came to Toronto as an adolescent in the early 1980s, as Augusto Pinochet entrenched his dictatorship. Without pressuring Bravo or her younger brother about maintaining Chilean culture, her parents simply held up the values of ousted president Salvador Allende's Popular Unity government as their own. 'I spent all my youth reading about ... fights against injustice,' says Bravo. 'Nothing shaped me more than this.' Her first personal step into public activism was taking part in Ryerson's long-running anti-racism radio show *Word of Mouth*.

Formerly vice-president of the Canadian Hispanic Congress, Bravo thinks advocating in our own backyards is as important as campaigning for a big-P party. Take schools, the institution

Alejandra Bravo

that most often convinces the politically reluctant to overcome their hesitations. Bravo's two sons go to Rawlinson Community School, where a disparate, multilingual group of parents came together, without staff support, to make sure meetings were held simultaneously in English, Spanish and Turkish. Soon the school will begin offering adult ESL classes, to make it even easier for parents to speak up for their children. 'We do a disservice to ourselves if we don't count that stuff,' Bravo says.

In 2006, Bravo made her second attempt at landing the City Council seat for Ward 17, Davenport, losing to incumbent Cesar Palacio by only 281 votes. Now, at Maytree, she runs the School for Civics program, which trains other hopeful City Hall newbies.

One school for civics grads

Sunny days spent playing cricket and soccer. Sounds like a kid's perfect summer, right? City rec centres try to keep fees low, but even a seemingly nominal $60 can be too much for a low-income family. Five years ago, Louroz Mercader saw that too many adolescents in his neighbourhood had nothing to do. So he got together with friends and created the Mississauga Youth Games.

Mercader lives in Cooksville, which is home to mostly South Asian, Chinese and Filipino families. He was born in Manila himself, and came to Canada at age four. Like many Filipinos, Mercader's dad works in a hotel, as a banquet manager; unlike far too many hotel workers, he has a unionized job at a decent wage. Mercader wants his neighbours to have job security and benefits, so he volunteers with the hotel workers' union Unite Here. He

wants his neighbours' children to
stay out of trouble, which is why
he started the Youth Games. Now
hundreds of kids spend their
summers playing sports, for free.

In 2010, the twenty-seven-
year-old ran for City Council in
Mississauga's Ward 7. He went up
against a twenty-two-year veteran
incumbent, Nando Iannicca, who
the Humber College grad says
hasn't reached out to recent

Louroz Mercader

newcomers. 'I think one reason voter turnout in Mississauga is low
is because we haven't engaged those communities,' says Mercader,
who listed safety, transit and a new BIA as his main issues.
Canada's only debt-free city is about 50 per cent non-white, but
you'd never know it looking at a photo of City Council. 'Somebody
has to take a leadership role,' Mercader says, 'and have the courage
to run.' Mercader came in second, after Iannicca, but he's determined to keep working and fighting on behalf of his community.

I see you

The loudest conversations about what 'matters' in this city stub-
bornly refuse to absorb Toronto as it really is. Yes, we need a more
diverse cast of elected characters, because that would give more
people a chance to participate in the upper echelons of civic life.
But real diversity would mean real change. Are you ready for that?
It's time to recognize that youth arts projects in Etobicoke benefit the whole city, and that if the participants have never visited
any big downtown arts institutions, it makes perfect sense that
they don't know why those places deserve humongous grants. If
the regularly scheduled food drives aren't bringing in the haul
that they used to, it's time to make sure that Ramadan donations

to the Daily Bread (which are pretty high, actually) get as much media fawning as what happens at Christmas. News media is facing a crisis worldwide, it's true, but what would happen to readership numbers in Toronto if our papers and magazines actually spoke to the population? The old scales and standards are outdated. Creating new ones isn't about 'fairness,' it's about reality. What's important to you is equally – and only – as essential to city life as what's important to anyone else.

In the summer of 2010, the Toronto Community Garden Network ran a program to unearth all the unheralded community food patches in the city, a nice acknowledgment of just how much work is happening off the radar. It's an excellent example of a centralized organization that stopped telling long enough to listen.

If the level of civic engagement sometimes looks bleak, maybe it's because we're looking at a picture that's way too small. All sorts of different people care very deeply about their communities, and their communities count. Think of the city, teeming with teenage soccer coaches, parent council chairs, adult literacy tutors, food-drive organizers, multilingual housing-support workers and neighbourhood gardeners, many of them from families that have been in the country for only a generation or two. They're all the public face of Toronto and any one of them could change the city's Public Face.

Get involved

acorncanada.org

artstarts.net

ivotetoronto.org

gashantiunity.ca

Denise Balkissoon has been published in the *Toronto Star*, the *Globe and Mail*, *EnRoute* and the *Boston Globe*, and has been nominated for multiple National Magazine Awards for her work with *Toronto Life*.

Jason McBride

A better world is possible

The Ontario Coalition Against Poverty and the
battle for the Special Diet Allowance

> Much of the violence associated with collective protest
> is the violence of authorities deploying force to restore
> normal institutional routines.
> — Frances Fox Piven, *Challenging Authority*

> But what is greater or braver than to beat down misfor-
> tune, or at least to try?
> — William T. Vollmann, *Poor People*

How do you end poverty? John Clarke carries that question
around like a child's chemistry set. On a bright Sunday morning in late June, Clarke, who's one of the founders of – and who,
despite his apparent reluctance, remains the face of – the
Ontario Coalition Against Poverty (OCAP), appeared at Ryerson
University on a panel called 'Resisting the G20: An Anti-
Capitalist Approach to Understanding and Resisting the G20
Agenda.'[1] The event was part of a weekend-long series of such
panels, workshops and discussions – the 2010 People's Summit
– that served as counter-programming to the G20 Summit
scheduled for the following weekend. The People's Summit was
insistently, even inspiringly, diverse, its expansive cluster of
more than one hundred events a crash course in contemporary
leftist politics. CUPE Ontario led a 'critical supermarket tour';
there was direct-action training and a DIY bike maintenance
course; various lectures and panels on animal rights, Islamo-
phobia, gun control and climate change were held.

1 The panel was held almost ten years to the day after OCAP's most notorious action
to date, the massive June 15, 2000, march on Queen's Park that drew about 1,500
people to the legislature and resulted in unprecedented violence (more on this later).

The 'Resisting the G20' panel, organized by a nascent activist group, the Greater Toronto Workers Assembly, was a generally placid, collegial gathering. Greg Albo, a York University political science professor, detailed, at length, the history of the G8 and G20 and, though he was reasonably animated and occasionally outraged, his lecture was no more dramatic than a grad school seminar. After a break, during which participants formed small discussion groups and mulled over Albo's arguments for several minutes, Clarke took a seat at the front of the room. The atmosphere instantly changed, as if a movie star (perhaps Campbell Scott, whom he resembles) had abruptly appeared and settled at the dais. Among friends and sympathizers, Clarke is affable and low-key, but most of those present had witnessed the fierce, eloquent invective he wields at marches and press conferences. This was not that particular version of Clarke, but he did permit his constantly simmering anger to regularly rise to the surface. 'There is no crisis so severe,' Clarke said drolly, speaking without notes, 'that the ruling class can't solve it at the expense of the working class.'

Clarke was born in Wimbledon, England, and, though he's been in Canada for almost forty years, his voice still bears its distinctive South London accent. He's fifty-six years old, slight though wiry (he's a runner) and, in the summer, dresses as if headed to the beach: T-shirts and polos, a pair of long shorts, sandals. He's still boyish, though his hair is silver and he wears cheap reading glasses that, when he's giving a talk, he peers over like a magistrate. He often punctuates his sentences with a kind of quick, conspiratorial smile – a nudge that lets you know he knows you know what he's saying, but that it bears repeating. And repeating again.

Clarke smiled frequently over the next half-hour as he expanded on what Albo called the coming austerity agenda, which most people in the room believed to be the ostensible focus of the G20 summit. Financial stimulus had, the argument went, largely restored the economies of, at least, the G8 nations, pulling each out of the recession. But for those same economies to avoid snapping back, new belt-tightening measures needed to be established, deficits cut, spending curtailed. In Ontario, such measures would, predictably, come at the expense of the poor and working classes – just as they had when Mike Harris came to power after the last major recession the province experienced.

Clarke's talk quickly found its focus: the Special Diet Allowance and OCAP's campaign around it, which has been at the heart of the organization's efforts to raise welfare rates. The Special Diet was a little-known program introduced in 2003 by Dalton McGuinty's Liberals. It allowed people on social assistance to receive a supplementary $250 a month to cover the cost of specific, generally more expensive food required by medical conditions (allergies, diabetes, etc.). The government barely promoted the program. Many welfare recipients were not even aware of it, though a majority of people on social assistance were eligible; simply and obviously put, if you can't afford even basic healthy food, which those on assistance cannot, you are much more likely to be sick or develop future illnesses. A single person on Ontario Works currently receives $595 per month.[2] If the

2 Such rates obviously don't allow a dignified, healthy life and they offer no opportunity for people to lift themselves out of poverty. Most are forced to make impossible choices between rent and food, medication and diapers, a transit pass or textbook. These rates mean that ever-increasing numbers of people are forced to rely on food banks, an emergency response that is now appallingly entrenched and institutionalized. Since 1995, food-bank use has grown by 80 per cent; since the beginning of the current recession, that number has risen an additional 20 per cent.

According to the Daily Bread Food Bank's most recent report, the number of client visits to food banks in the last year was 1,187,000. Of those visitors, 34 per cent were children. And 45 per cent of food bank clients have a serious illness or are disabled. Ontario social assistance cases grew by 11 per cent between January 2009 and January 2010, though they decreased slightly – by about 1,000 cases – in the summer of 2010.

average rent for a bachelor apartment in Toronto is $800, there's not much left for a healthy diet. Indeed, in a national health study, StatsCan determined that one-fifth of the poor suffered from three or more chronic conditions, and that, in Ontario, poor women are four times as likely to get diabetes as rich women.

OCAP saw the Special Diet as a way for those on assistance to take back some of the money cut by the Harris government[3] in the mid-'90s – a situation not remedied by McGuinty despite his government's much-ballyhooed poverty reduction strategy.[4] And, in 2005, OCAP started doing exactly what the government was not: telling people about the Special Diet. Over 100 health-care professionals and experts signed a letter saying that all Ontario Works and Ontario Disability Support Program recipients should be entitled to the full supplement on a permanent basis due to the inadequacy of welfare rates. The Daily Bread Food Bank, the country's largest food bank, soon followed suit.

In the budget handed down in March 2010, however, Finance Minister Dwight Duncan announced that the program

3 Harris downloaded some costs of social services to municipalities in 1998. Ontario is the only Canadian province that still requires a direct municipal government contribution towards the cost of providing welfare to those residing within municipal boundaries. Municipalities pay 20 per cent of total OW and ODSP bills, though the City administers the former and the provincial government the latter. In a 2008 announcement that both heartened and dismayed critics (heartened that it was announced at all, dismayed because of its tardiness), the Liberals declared that the cost of ODSP will be gradually transferred to the provincial government between 2009 and 2011, and that all welfare benefit costs will be uploaded by 2018 (a savings to Ontario's municipalities of $400 million a year).

4 In fact, in real terms, welfare recipients are much worse off under the provincial Liberals than they were under Harris. Harris cut assistance rates by almost 22 per cent in 1995, but the Liberals' scant increases in rates – about 6 per cent since 2003 – have obviously not restored those cuts, nor even kept pace with inflation or increases in the cost of living. In the last budget, rates were raised by 1 per cent – approximately the cost of a single round-trip TTC ride per month – while inflation was projected to rise by 2 per cent.

was being cancelled and replaced with a new medical supplement administered by the Ministry of Health. In a statement, OCAP declared that 'the elimination of the Special Diet Benefit will result in a 3 per cent cut to the income of poor people on social assistance.[5] This is only the third time in Ontario history that a government has slashed income to the poor – Hepburn did it in '38, Harris in '95, and McGuinty in the 2010 Budget.' As of this writing, details about the new program, or precisely when it will be introduced, have not been revealed. It's expected, however, that the program will provide only a fraction of what the Special Diet provided. 'The worst-case scenario is some people will get some protein powder, with a great deal of scrutiny,' says Clarke.

As Clarke's presentation was winding down, his ire only increased. He concluded, characteristically, on a full-throated, mocking note of provocation, that, once again, lit the fuse for future action. 'I do believe a better world is possible,' he said. 'But how do you convince poor people of this if you can't stop a rat-faced git like Dalton McGuinty from taking away their groceries?'

OCAP's very name pits it explicitly against poverty, but who would say, equally as explicitly, that they are *for* poverty? Clarke argues that government does, that it necessarily requires the continued existence of the poor and that its policies reflect that dismal fact. Government, whether led by Mike Harris, Dalton McGuinty or David Miller, serves only the interests of the wealthy ruling class. And a ruling class, by definition, needs to have somebody to rule.

Clarke's logic is that Ontario's current economy requires both an ever-growing supply of low-wage and minimum-wage earners and that welfare therefore must be kept so appallingly,

5 This past year, food banks experienced a 15 per cent increase, the largest rise in client visits since 1995, when assistance rates were cut by 22 per cent.

impossibly low and its attainment so punitive and degrading, that it becomes no choice at all. 'Exceptionally exploitative employment had to remain the better option for the poor,' Clarke has written. 'The refinement of the system that is now being prepared provides a subsidy to low-wage employers, a sub-standard benefit for children on assistance and a way of isolating and dealing harshly with employable adults.'

OCAP was founded as a way for those who are oppressed by this ruling class to disrupt and agitate it. As Jonah Schein, a social worker and OCAP member, has put it, 'Unlike the social agencies in which we work, OCAP positions itself as marginal and outside the system that enforces injustice.' One of Clarke's inspirations was – and continues to be – *Poor People's Movements: Why They Succeed, How They Fail*, published in 1977 by American academics Frances Fox Piven and Richard Cloward. 'Right from the start, we wanted to avoid being a concerned citizens' organization, a lobbying voice,' says Clarke. 'Our perspective has always been one of social mobilization. This is the formulation that Piven and Cloward put forward: that the main way the poor can have political influence is through their ability to create crises by disrupting institutions.'

Clarke was a laid-off Westinghouse factory worker and former union shop steward in London, Ontario, when he joined the London Union of Unemployed Workers in the late 1980s. He helped organize a march on Queen's Park, which drew together workers from across the province to demand that David Peterson's Liberal government make good on an increase in welfare rates recommended by its own review committee. The action was hugely successful – the Liberals eventually raised rates by 9 per cent, among other things – and the march's participants realized that a permanent province-wide coalition against poverty might be possible. The major unions, the Canadian Union of Public Employees and the Canadian Auto

Workers, provided seed money. At the outset, the organization committed to mobilizing the poor and homeless to fight back through militant, direct action, eschewing any notion of consultation or compromise with those in power. Just as OCAP was being formed and Clarke chosen as its leader,[6] the province headed into an election. OCAP relentlessly harassed Peterson on the campaign trail (he was dubbed the 'Poverty Premier'); then–New Democratic Party leader Bob Rae would eventually win the election.

OCAP and a new, left-leaning NDP government were therefore born almost simultaneously. But if they were ostensible siblings, their relationship immediately took on a Cain-and-Abel cast. OCAP repeatedly accused Rae and his ministers of failing to live up to their own promises of welfare reform. Confused by the disappointments of a seemingly natural ally, OCAP devoted its energies to more tangible, grassroots casework like preventing evictions, stopping deportations and fighting for denied wages. The organization also turned its anger upon the federal Tories – in one infamous action, a tent city, 'Mulroneyville,' was built outside the Metro Convention Centre during a PC convention.

When Rae was eventually defeated by Mike Harris, however, the organization at last found its true, and most despised, target. Unlike either Peterson or Rae, Harris unapologetically demonized the poor, and his onerous policies – amalgamation, criminalizing panhandling, granting landlords more power and, of course, cutting welfare rates – provided OCAP with many fronts

6 Clarke is OCAP's only full-time paid employee. Despite his disdain for 'the cult of personality' and his reluctance to assume the mantle of leadership, it's difficult to deny how large a role he's played in the organization's success. He's a showman, an expert at media relations, and while he's been insistent about shifting the focus on to other OCAP organizers like Gaetan Heroux, Stefan Pilipa and Liisa Schofield, Clarke's charisma and uncompromising militancy has completely coloured, even shaped, the organization's complexion.

on which to do battle. As its constituencies became more fearful and desperate, OCAP became increasingly aggressive: it set
up a four-day-long tent city in Allan Gardens called 'Safe Park';
it launched a mass panhandle at the gala premiere of the Toronto
International Film Festival (filmmaker Atom Egoyan subse-
quently, if absurdly, dedicated the evening 'to the homeless'); a
hundred very vocal people marched through Cabbagetown to
protest closing shelters and drop-ins under the guise of 'cleans-
ing' the neighbourhood.

Finally, on June 15, 2000, OCAP launched the largest
demonstration in its history. Assembling 1,500 people from
across the province on the lawn at Queen's Park, OCAP demanded
that a small delegation of poor people be allowed to directly
address the legislature. The crowd moved towards the barri-
cades and an immense police presence. While expecting to be
denied entry, Clarke still anticipated that things would end in
peaceful discussion. They didn't. Barriers were overturned, the
legislature rushed. Pepper spray clouded the air; a firebomb
went off. Protesters hurled paving stones and mounted police
retaliated with nightsticks. By the end of the day, forty-two police
officers had been injured, ten horses hurt and dozens of demon-
strators arrested. The event was dubbed the Queen's Park Riot.
Clarke was later arrested and released on bail, on the condition
that he not attend any more demonstrations, go within 500
metres of Queen's Park or have any contact with OCAP.

Such constraints did not deter him. A year later, he joined
a group of fifty OCAP members and occupied Finance Minister
Jim Flaherty's office in Whitby, trashing furniture. Clarke was
arrested again[7] and spent twenty-five days in the Whitby jail,

7 There's not space here to detail Clarke's subsequent legal battles. Suffice it to say,
throughout the early 2000s, Clarke spent much time in court defending himself
against 'masterminding' the Queen's Park Riot. In late October 2003, the case was
finally closed and OCAP, in many ways, redeemed.

without bail. The Crown attorney described his behaviour as 'an act of terrorism.' OCAP became, to some minds, radioactive. Public and union support for the organization began to waver. Some social agencies with whom OCAP shared common goals and sensibilities distanced themselves. To many, Clarke was the problem, and OCAP's close association with him – the two are almost synonymous for some people – resulted in some loss of support for the organization. From both sides of the political spectrum, in fact: Mel Lastman famously called Clarke a 'thug,' and both *NOW Magazine* and *Socialist Worker* took up editorial arms against him. Rabble-rousing, it seemed, was fine, but there was a thin line between respectable rabble-rouser and unrepentant ruffian.

A decade later, such actions still largely characterize OCAP in the public's mind. This is misleading and unfair. While the organization has hardly stepped back from militant action and dramatic street theatre – as I was writing this, Clarke was arrested again, along with ten others, after forcibly entering Liberal headquarters to deliver an invoice 'demanding full repayment of benefits taken from people living on social assistance' – OCAP spends much more of its time and resources on concrete, localized casework that receives scant media attention but which can short-circuit bureaucratic processes that are often extremely lengthy and costly[8] – 'what's immediately

8 A somewhat digressive anecdote: at the time of this writing, I work part-time for the Stop Community Food Centre, which has also been involved in improving social-assistance rates, most visibly in a campaign called 'Do the Math.' As successful as that campaign has been in drawing attention to the issue – and Clarke spoke admiringly to me about the Stop's work in general – the change it was possibly effecting was proceeding far too slowly for some, in particular those who had been receiving the Special Diet. 'People are dying,' one frail woman said, visibly anguished. She never came to another meeting. OCAP's appeal, for some, is how quickly, decisively and angrily it can respond to policy issues. Unaccountable to government or wealthy donors, it's free to operate in a nimble, risky manner.

possible,' in Clarke's words: ensuring that shelter spaces are kept open, for example, or that repairs are made to public housing, or that welfare cheques arrive on time. OCAP's unglamorous but wholly necessary work in the streets is what has allowed it to create deep roots in poor communities. It puts food in bellies, roofs over heads, hope in hearts. It's what gets people to come to meetings and demonstrations.

OCAP's direct-action casework operates according to three principles: combining legal work with disruptive action (picketing a gas station, for example, that's failed to properly pay its employees); not duplicating the work done by conventional legal clinics (which OCAP views as often ineffective and discouraging); and forwarding political goals without compromising the interests of those being worked with (the idea being that in each case, the aggrieved party is able to fully see the power a small group of people can wield – but not at the expense of their winning their case). In its early days, OCAP's casework involved only welfare offices and their often inscrutable, arbitrary systems, and it was extremely successful – to the point now that the organization usually needs only to fax a letter or make a call to get someone's cheque released. OCAP's had similar results at shelters (where people have had their property stolen) and in preventing illegal evictions. (It's been less successful working Children's Aid cases or in prisons, where physical disruption is obviously much more difficult.)

The tools of this casework are unremarkable – no Molotov cocktails here – and common to any conventional office: a phone, a fax machine and organizers with adequate free time to devote to cases, as well as some basic legal knowledge. More difficult to provide, however, and something that OCAP tries to ensure before taking on a case (OCAP's notoriety has helped in this regard; its reputation, as well as outreach through like-minded agencies, has ensured a steady supply of cases), is confidence that the case is winnable. And then the route to such victory follows a fairly similar pattern: a letter, outlining the legal grounds for any demands, is sent to a high-ranking official. If it seems public action might be needed, then it's made explicit that such will be undertaken if demands are not met. This usually means bringing a delegation to the appropriate office with a demand to speak to a supervisor rather than a caseworker or others who do not have the power to intervene. If this meeting is not granted, the delegation disrupts the regular workings of the office, escalating these disruptions until the meeting is granted. Offices are often 'hit' over and over again. The number of people brought out to an action depends on what numbers are needed to be effective; it can vary from fewer than half a dozen at some welfare actions to over a hundred people at some immigration actions.[9]

OCAP has no formal membership system, but there are roughly a hundred people who are active on a constant basis and several thousand throughout the city who operate on the periphery of the organization, attending occasional actions. There is an elected executive committee of ten people, which meets every two weeks (as does the membership). The executive plans strategy and makes recommendations to the general membership. Ad hoc working groups are formed on given issues. OCAP's annual operating budget oscillates between $60,000 and $80,000, and the bulk of that money comes from private donations. Union donations, once OCAP's bread and butter, have recently begun to return. (As the car industry continues its decline, and increasing numbers of the CAW join the welfare rolls, the union's national leadership, not surprisingly, has begun to look favourably upon OCAP again.) Anyone can join OCAP – one need but show up at an action or call (416-925-6939) to find out when the next meeting is – though the organization, which

9 These details are all taken from OCAP's Direct Action Casework Manual.

insists that it 'believes in the power of people to organize them-selves,' tends to casually recruit from the very constituency it serves and outreaches to: the poor, unemployed and those on social assistance.[10]

In terms of strategy and decision-making, OCAP insists stren-uously on inclusivity and transparency; it's organizing not for the poor, but by the poor. But one of the most obvious challenges in organizing the poor is that the poor are no less self-interested and apathetic than anyone else. At the same time, the unbear-able deprivations of unemployment, welfare and homelessness can be isolating and stigmatizing; they actively discourage and disable collective action. 'I have to admit that the rich are more class-conscious than the poor,' Clarke says. 'That's the greatest barrier. But you can only overcome it by giving a lead and doing long, patient, consistent work in communities.'

The Special Diet has arguably been the most successful of this consistent work. When OCAP learned of the program, in early 2005, it pounced. What many dismissed as a loophole, OCAP strategically saw as a pressure point. The Special Diet was part of provincial welfare and disability policy. In other words, a government-approved Special Diet would be prescribed by a medical provider and then Ontario Works and the Ontario Disability Support Program would be required to pay the allowance. People on assistance could, for the first time, afford a little meat or fresh fruit. Thousands of people signed up for the Special Diet at OCAP's 'Hunger Clinics,' held in community centres, parks and apartment buildings across the province. Medical providers filled out the notoriously complex, opaque

10 As is often the case, there's a tendency to romanticize the militant left – even this essay is guilty of this, to a degree – but critics, even largely sympathetic ones, of OCAP have voiced concern about its holier-than-thou insularity. A few people have complained privately to me about OCAP's resistance to help from both those outside its usual circles and those deemed not sufficiently invested in the struggle.

forms for patients; translators were on hand for non-English speakers. On one day in October 2005, more than a thousand people showed up at Queen's Park for an enormous Hunger Clinic (complete with childcare and a large meal) featuring forty medical providers, set up in wooden cubicles, who filled out Special Diet forms that eventually netted recipients $3 million extra in benefits. By 2009, the program had ballooned to $200 million from just $6 million in 2003.

Even with these impressive numbers, Clarke points out, there has been little media interest in the Special Diet fight. Indeed, after McGuinty became provincial leader, OCAP – so ironically wed to Mike Harris, at least in the public's mind – became less visible. This is likely due to the fact that, generally speaking, Liberal policy isn't as obviously and explicitly opposed to the welfare state as Tory policy typically is. But OCAP became a more visible force during the recent recession.

Beyond delivering tangible help to many on assistance, the Special Diet also allowed OCAP to develop relationships with communities it had never before attempted to organize. Toronto's Somali community – disproportionately impoverished and generally having escaped massive political and social upheaval – became involved when a couple of its members volunteered their translation services at Hunger Clinics. In April 2006, a group of Somali women formed an office of their own – the OCAP Women of Etobicoke – and became an integral and highly visible part of the organization's actions. They marched on Rosedale, took on a security firm that had been harassing Somali youth and assisted each other in obtaining benefits that had been denied. Traditionally tasked with the resettlement of their often very large families, these women were daily confronting the frustrations and caprices of civic institutions; they likewise weren't always aware of the rights they were entitled to. Their association with OCAP permitted them a previously impossible level of civic engagement while providing OCAP itself with a new and diverse roster of activists. 'The money from welfare was not enough,' said one of the Somali organizers, Amina Ali, in a 2006 interview. 'Whatever you get goes to the rent, and then the rest – maybe fifty bucks – has to last. You know how stressful it is when you don't know what you're going to feed your kids tomorrow. It's not healthy.' The Special Diet campaign enabled OCAP to vividly show how entwined poverty and health truly are. The point of the Special Diet campaign is that all recipients of social assistance require and deserve that extra bit of money because living on the meagre amounts afforded by assistance means their health is undeniably imperiled and, over time, will only become worse. Stress, hypertension, diabetes and heart disease will all increase because the only food welfare recipients can afford is often utterly lacking in nutritional value.

As valuable as the Special Diet was to so many on Ontario Works and ODSP – more than 136,000 at last count[11] – the program's entire history has been marred by increasingly cruel bureaucratic interference. Some welfare offices tried to turn down applications that had been signed by qualified practitioners. The City of Toronto – which administers the program on behalf of the province – embarked on an additional review of all Special Diet cases and, a couple years later, forced applicants to sign a form that entitled OW to access their medical records, including psychiatric reports, sexual history and any other private information that their doctors had on file. At the end of 2005, provincial Social Services Minister Sandra Pupatello, claiming that people were 'cheating the system' – and singling out OCAP's efforts – slashed the program, making it much more difficult for anyone to receive the monthly supplement. The program allowed medical

11 As *Toronto Star* reporter Catherine Porter has pointed out, this is only 16 per cent of the people receiving social assistance. Where are the rest?

providers to diagnose only from a list of forty-three specific medical conditions, and those patients suffering from such conditions, in turn, received grossly inadequate amounts. Serious heart and liver conditions, for example, resulted in measly payments of $10 a month. Allowances were drastically reduced in most cases. Complaints against the changes were launched through the Ontario Human Rights Commission, and this year the commission found the Liberal government's changes to the diet allowance were discriminatory.[12] Then, as mentioned earlier, after a 2009 Auditor General's report questioned the legitimacy of some people receiving the diet allowance, the McGuinty government has now finally decided to scrap the program altogether.[13]

12 I quote the decision in part here: 'Over the past two years, hundreds of human rights complaints were made that the Special Diet Allowance for people on Ontario Works Assistance or the Ontario Disability Support Program was discriminatory because it excluded some disabilities and allowed not enough money for others. To deal with this large volume of cases, the Tribunal decided to hear three "lead" cases and to apply the lessons learned to the other cases ... In its decision in February 2010, the Tribunal found that the program discriminated against the complainants by excluding certain medical conditions and providing relatively unequal amounts for other conditions ... The Tribunal ordered retroactive benefits for the three complainants from the date that they would have been eligible for them if the discrimination had not happened. The Tribunal also ordered the government to provide special diet benefits for people with hypoproteinemia, hyperlipidemia, hypertension and obesity within three months of the decision. This decision is facing a court challenge, and the Province has proposed to eliminate the program and begin a new one through the Ministry of Health and Long-Term Care. In the meantime, the OHRC and various partners continue to negotiate with the Province to move forward with the other special diet cases.'

13 The most infamous example of this chronic and patronizing governmental capriciousness – you might liken it to a parent who gives a child candy with one hand and then slaps her with the other – is the case of Dr. Roland Wong. Wong, a compassionate OCAP ally, sympathetic to the plight of welfare recipients, was brought before the College of Physicians and Surgeons for allegedly falsifying Special Diet forms. In January of this year, he appeared at a hearing to determine if his medical licence should be revoked. It wasn't. In a speech Wong gave in April 2010, he said, 'Income level is the best predictor of health ... More will die as McGuinty's misguided policies continue to suffocate the poor.' It eventually came to light that the city councillor who learned of and 'exposed' Wong was Rob Ford.

'The effect of the Special Diet campaign has been enormous,' Clarke says. 'But to put it in perspective, we were only able to get back about 10 per cent of what was taken away from people [after the Harris cuts]. So we're in no position to be complacent.'

A week after the 'Resisting the G20' panel, Clarke stood again in front of a crowd of roughly 2,000 people in Allan Gardens. It was Friday, June 25, the beginning of the G20 Summit. The park was ringed with police, part of a $1 billion security force that had been relentlessly denigrated by the groups that had gathered there. As I entered the park, a York Region officer said to me, while illegally searching my knapsack, 'It's a beautiful day for a protest. A peaceful protest.'

It was. OCAP had organized the march that day along with dozens of other activist groups, including No One Is Illegal, Jane and Finch Action Against Poverty, South Asian Women's Rights Organization and People for Climate Justice – the first time such an eclectic array of activists had collaborated on an action. Despite the inordinate presence of riot police – immense phalanxes occupied every alley and sidewalk – it was entirely peaceful. The march snaked along Carlton and College, only to be stymied at University Avenue, where, after a relatively mild confrontation with police, protestors turned back towards the park. There, as evening fell, about fifty people put up tents. Later reports criticized the march for lacking a single overarching issue, as if a coalition of concerns were an automatic detriment rather than a possible advantage. The mainstream media wanted a message, but not more than one, or not one that was too complex. At the same time, it ignored the fact that this plurality of issues had its roots in the obvious, single-minded anger focused on the general policies of the G20 itself. But the media's dismissal was dumbfounding throughout the G20 weekend. It largely avoided real, frightening stories of constitutional abuse and illegal policing in favour of stories of black-clad, youthful marauders who were less violent than the hockey fans who'd razed Montreal the month previously.

The real story for Clarke, however, was the momentum the weekend produced. 'People felt that the G20 needed to be challenged,' he says. 'Thousands of people stayed on the streets all day Saturday, all day Sunday. And then, on Monday, they went back to police headquarters, where they might have been walking into a violent trap. It was remarkable.' Clarke mentions, with some amusement, that a few days after the G20, OCAP held an open house for those who had been affected by the weekend's events. An impoverished Mexican woman who had been arrested came expressly because a cop told her she'd be released if she promised to have nothing to do with OCAP – an organization that, until then, she had never heard of.

Clarke holds out hope that the groups with which OCAP organized the Friday march, No One Is Illegal and Coalition Against Israeli Apartheid, will join forces in a common front of organizations that, broadly speaking, have an anti-capitalist perspective. He's also hopeful that the socialist Workers Assembly, with several members in various trade unions, can build an inter-union alliance that will influence the political complexion of their respective locals. All of this is possible, he says, within even just a few months. 'I won't say it's likely,' he says, smiling. 'But there is a real possibility.'

'Possibility' is one of Clarke's favourite words. And the large social movement that he envisions does seem, at least when you're in his presence, possible. Walking with the G20 protestors – a far more diverse, caring and generous population than was depicted in most newspapers and TV reports – also makes such possibility plausible. Even ending poverty seems possible. How? Just one example: there's enough empty heated, carpeted office space in Toronto, Clarke argues, to house the entire homeless population. Obviously, he says, living in office buildings isn't a long-term solution, but this fact illustrates that, in Canada, at least, wealth and resources are plentiful – it's just their distribution that's inequitable. 'I don't think poverty is necessary,' Clarke says. 'It's designed, it's imposed, it's even legislated. But it's not inevitable.'

Get involved
www.ocap.ca

Thanks to Jonah Schein for generously sharing his writings on OCAP with me.

Jason McBride is a Toronto-based writer and editor and a regular contributor to *Toronto Life*, the *Globe and Mail*, *Cinema Scope* and *The Believer*. He is also communications coordinator at the Stop Community Food Centre.

Hannah Sung
Rap sheet to rap record
Harnessing the power of music

Everyone wants to make a difference, but how? Where to begin? The second hand ticks down through messy workdays as we run to meetings, field calls, put out fires at the office, slump off to bed – in other words, our days get filled with life. Ideals get shunted aside. Volunteer time, if it happens at all, gets reduced to near nothing.

That said, there are individuals who shape their lives around making a difference. Their messy workdays, their errands and calls, all revolve around creating positive social change.

One such person is Tamara Dawit. She is immensely effective at creating social-issues education, or 'edutainment,' that cuts through the clutter of information and misinformation aimed at young people to deliver useful wisdom. Her story may impart some directional advice for those who want to follow the same path towards creating community change; like most stories, it also involves many of the people around her. So we'll begin with myself, then head to jail and, finally, we'll get to how it all began and why it works.

I first met Tamara as a reporter covering a high school presentation she mounted in 2005 with her non-profit, the 411 Initiative for Change. She brings rappers, musicians and poets into schools, engaging students by speaking their rhythmic language and creating a spectacle. Each time she enters a school, she gifts students with an unexpected experience that obliterates notions of boring guest-speaker assemblies. Rappers, skilled at playing clubs and working cool crowds into a lather, work stages in school auditoriums and in junior high gymnasiums, spitting fire on topics such as HIV/AIDS or women's rights. Kids, as you would imagine, love it.

Years later, I found myself joining her travelling pack, hosting school assemblies across several provinces with rappers Rochester and Eternia. It was an experience in watching young junior high and high school students literally grow before my eyes. School after school, I watched the kids go from being, in school terms, well-behaved, which means passive and quiet, to being goaded into the call-and-response of rap participation. Every time, they left charged with new information and energy, more than a few of them with moony eyes for the performers who'd left their sweat on the stage.

From the first time I saw her 411 performances, I've been convinced of Tamara's amazing ability to create change.

I reconnected with Tamara in early 2010 on a crisp, spring morning. To get the latest on the 411, we were going to head to jail.

Cobourg, Ontario, is a small town about an hour east of Toronto. We're visitors to Brookside, a place that admin call a 'youth centre.' The young men here call it 'jail.' They're here because they have made giant missteps in life – they've committed, or are charged with committing, serious crimes including rape, murder, drugs and firearms offences. Many have made the same trek I did, from Toronto to Cobourg. Brookside is both close to and far from the world they know at home, and staff take care to watch for too much pride of place, which can turn into turf battles brought into Brookside from the outside world.

Upon entering, visitors must surrender phones, wallets and personal effects at central security before heading through a series of locked gates; the sprawling grounds are fenced in by chain-link that stretches high into the sky. The complex looks like a summer camp drained of colour, with a scattering of low, brown institutional buildings linked by paved paths. The trees are still bare at this time of year, the grass scrappy. At one end of the property, I'm guided down a stairwell to a subterranean classroom. Within Brookside the 'jail,' there is Brookside the school, and the classroom I enter is nondescript, with aging posters of '70s rock bands on the walls that surely weren't put there by the kids themselves. This is where I meet a handful of students who are taking part in an innovative music program.

I come through this door with an entourage Tamara has brought together, including a music producer, a graphic designer, a rap artist and the school's vice-principal, Louise Nadeau, who is leading the pack. There are two youth services officers in the room who act as guards. Also in the classroom, an educational assistant and the music teacher herself, Joanne Drury.

At once, after the music professionals and the students exchange hand slaps and greetings, they set about turning this classroom into an impromptu music studio. We are the unlikeliest people in the unlikeliest place to witness the birth of a rap album.

Five students at Brookside were selected for the Rebirth Project, a ten-week workshop that began in January 2010. Tamara has used her wide-reaching connections to gather a group of music industry professionals to mentor the students, producing two singles they've written and recorded themselves. They even design the album art. Like every other classroom at Brookside, the music room is a safe place, where teachers don't know, and don't want to know, what students have done to bring them to Brookside. It's how everyone can concentrate on learning, by having the boys check their criminal pasts at the door.

The week I visit, they are in their eighth workshop class, deep into the process of writing and recording. In the classroom, I watch students use Photoshop to create album art that obscures their identity (they agree on silhouette images) because they, contrary to hip-hop braggadocio, are not allowed to identify themselves. While living out their rap dream, they still have to work within the Young Offenders Act.

Daniel and his friend Gary, two participants in the Rebirth Project, are not in class today. They've been suspended for several weeks for getting into a fight. As they relayed it to admin, rumours swirled among the boys that Daniel and Gary would be attacked after class earlier in the week, but the two teens didn't report the rumours. Instead, when they were indeed attacked, they fought back, which resulted in an automatic twenty-day suspension from class for everyone involved. Suspended students do get their school work brought to them after five days, but the suspension is a necessary consequence.

Being suspended for twenty days means Gary and Daniel are shut out of the classroom during the carefully scheduled time when they were to finally record their raps. School admin were reluctant to take the boys out of class so close to the completion of the project – vice-principal Nadeau called it 'heartbreaking' – but rules are rules.

The irony of Brookside is that, for those who find themselves there, it has the potential to be the best thing to happen to them. A fast life of criminal behaviour can be rerouted by an experience like Brookside, where young offenders are taken out of their home environment and given an opportunity to refocus on school. However, there are distractions. Of the five students in the Rebirth Project, Daniel and Gary were jumped and suspended, one student recently found out his brother died, another had high hopes for his immediate future dashed when a court hearing was cancelled by his lawyer for no discernible reason. When a lab instrument went missing in a science class earlier in the week, the school was on lockdown while students were searched. Distractions may be a regular part of high school life, but this is extreme.

The students have an exceptional music teacher in Joanne Drury, a middle-aged woman with a sweet, open expression.

Her students adore her. She wears keys on a lanyard around her neck and sensible running shoes. Through her students, she has learned to appreciate rap. For years, she didn't allow hip hop in class. Then she realized this was the way her students were going to express themselves – through music. She enlisted the help of an outside friend, an OPP officer with expertise in gangs, to make sure she could understand the language of the streets and have the tools necessary to keep rhymes positive in the classroom. Her appreciation for the lyricism of rap has now evolved to the point where she is at the helm of a class rap record.

While the remaining three students are recording in class with Joanne and the 411 mentors, I meet with Daniel in a cramped interview room. Even when slumped in his chair, Daniel has the bulk of a very large kid, a tall shock of hair making him even bigger. The room is spare, and we sit across from each other as he fidgets, a youth services officer stationed outside the door. Daniel is wearing head-to-toe burgundy fleece, standard-issue black running shoes and the apprehensive expression of a child unsure of what the adult is about to say. He is an eighteen-year-old portrait of clashes, a jumbled mix of vulnerability and raw power.

'How long have you been rapping?' I ask.

He tells me he's been doing it since he was six or seven, when he'd drop rhymes for his mom, making her laugh. 'I don't think they were bad,' he qualifies. 'She just found them funny.'

I ask him to rap for me. Without hesitation, he draws a breath and launches into several verses. As he raps, his frame, already oversized, begins to grow before my eyes.

Ducking and weaving around a silent beat, he name-drops Ne-Yo, the Matrix and Kriss Kross, cracking jokes and allusions in rapid succession. What his mom says is true. He *is* funny. When he's done, I nod appreciatively. He says, 'Thank you, thank you,' like he's onstage, no longer in an inquisition. He admits that his singular ambition in life is to become a rap star.

Becoming a huge rap star isn't very likely in Canada, even for someone young, gifted and black. Stardom just doesn't strike that often. I'm not sure if Daniel knows this or even cares, but what's obvious from his performance in this dingy room is that rapping energizes and enlivens him. Being witty and rapping his story is how he can, for a moment, get closer to his dream. For those of us who believe being a rap superstar may be a pipe dream, it occurs to me that for some of the young men at Brookside, stability and opportunity may seem just as far-fetched.

Daniel switches places with Gary, also sitting out this week's workshop, who's next in line to meet with me. Gary is quieter, with a baby face and hair in corn rows. He tells me about learning storytelling skills a few weeks earlier with Toronto spoken-word artist and poet Motion. The session inspired Gary to write out his life story, something he'd never done before. He says he clearly saw the moment where things started 'to go wrong.' He mused about possibly rapping it for his mom on the phone.

Gary and Daniel are obviously in love with everything about hip hop. But the Rebirth Project, as it turns out, is about more than rap.

'It's not about teaching them how to become a rapper,' Tamara tells me later, in her trademark matter-of-fact style. 'The original intention was to improve on basic skills, like interpersonal skills. These are students working together who would normally have never even spoken to each other,' she says of the five young men. 'These are students who, in the past, could not trust adults they were working with.'

For the boys, this workshop goes back only a few weeks, but for Brookside and the 411, it goes back a year, during which they manoeuvred to bring the Rebirth Program to fruition, navigating a lengthy process of accessing Ontario arts grants. At just thirty years old, Tamara has gained considerable experience in funding her projects. That's because she began the 411 when she was still in high school herself.

To this day, more than ten years later, she is still DIY. At times, she has the budget to pay one full-time employee, plus she has the occasional student intern. Other than that, it's all her. She is able to accomplish what she does by surrounding herself with talented young people who want to give back to their communities. Besides producing multimedia performance tours that are presented in high schools across Canada to raise student awareness about Black History Month, AIDS/HIV, girls' and women's rights, she has also co-produced special TV programming in partnership with MTV Canada, sending on-air hosts and musicians to Sudan, Colombia and Haiti, so that Canadian audiences can tag along for a first-person view of the challenges their peers face around the world.

On any given day, Tamara looks more like a student than admin. On this day in Cobourg, she's wearing a hoodie, jeans, hoop earrings and boots with fur tassels. Her black hair hangs in waves to her shoulders. She has a killer smile but flashes it only occasionally. She is unafraid to deliver blunt truths. On the day I visit, she addresses the three remaining students, taking each aside individually for feedback on the program. They are all curious about how she came to be here in their class; the respect they have for her is evident. One student asks her if she 'owns' this program and how she became 'the boss.' Tamara explains it in a nutshell, making sure to take it back to the beginning, as she does for me later that week at her office in east-end Toronto, a space shared with other young creative professionals, all white walls, tall ceilings, exposed pipes and bikes hung upside down on the wall.

'I wanted to produce Black History Month programming in my [Ottawa] high school because I was facing a lot of racism in school,' Tamara explains. 'I was one of three or four black kids.' She says her experience in high school involved racist bullying and messages drawn on her locker – threats serious enough for police to become involved.

Tamara Dawit

Tamara used her outrage to fuel her actions. She was, as she puts it, 'motivated by being pissed off.'

Once the school principal approved her initiative as a school club, she began organizing her school's first Black History Month assembly. 'I thought that perhaps doing this type of programming would make it easier for other kids,' she says. The few other black students in school didn't join, but her closest girlfriends, who just happened to be white, did. Together, they publicized Tamara's project with posters around the school. She also jumped on the availability of the school's public address system, as every student club leader had access to it. She had a local college radio station DJ make mixes of her favourite political gangsta rap artists – Gravediggaz, NWA, Ice Cube, Ice T, Public Enemy – asking him to take out any bad language. When her DJ contact was too busy to make mixes, she would cut and paste songs herself, using two tape decks, recording cassette-to-cassette. These songs would get played in the mornings and between classes. Finally, her peers at school gathered for her Black History Month assembly.

'The guest speaker was an academic who spoke on racist practices related to the immigration of people of African descent into Canada,' she reminisces. The presentation also involved poetry, an African drummer and a speech by an elderly woman who had been a student at one of the first integrated schools in Montreal. As Tamara tells it, her peers were thoroughly bored.

'They found it boring or they were busy making fun of the older lady and her outfit,' she says. 'They weren't retaining information because they were tuning out.'

Tamara took it in stride and tried again the next year.

'We incorporated pop culture and talked about more contemporary issues in 1999. We decided to expand the program,' she says, citing a school-board equity program she discovered. She worked with them to get a theatre director, a sound tech and a community centre as a space for rehearsals. She held auditions for volunteer performers, culled from the African-Canadian community active in an organization called Black History Ottawa. Tamara's goal aligned with that of Black History Ottawa in that they all wanted to make sure there was programming in schools for Black History Month. Still in high school, Tamara was learning the importance of partnering organizations towards a common goal.

Tamara wrote up a performance piece that year. 'The historical issues were embedded in the play, so it was more digestible,' she says. She scored a sponsorship through BMG and Universal record labels, which gave her enough swag for modest trivia prize packs at school.

Tamara's second Black History Month assembly was a pop-culturally savvy affair. It became a traveller, with plans to visit nine schools, including a special performance at the University of Ottawa, all within one week.

Unwittingly, she was now well on her way towards what would become a career in producing educational entertainment events. But at that moment, her most important order of business was to fill an immediate, practical need: her band of volunteers needed to get around.

'We were sponsored by the public bus system,' she says. Ottawa's West Indian Transit Club, an association of West Indian bus drivers, was her 'in': they offered sponsorship and access to a free city bus for the week, the drivers offering their time, their bosses agreeing to lend the bus as long as the gas and drivers' time was covered. Tamara convinced the drivers to volunteer their time. Gas came to about $300 and she remembers it as being their single biggest expense that year.

She had a budget of $1000, which came from developing a relationship with the Canadian Race Relations Foundation that year. Besides the cost of gas, there was a rental fee for the space at U of O and some printing and miscellaneous expenses. Tamara and the Canadian Race Relations Foundation still work together today.

Her Black History Month assembly grew into an event for the public when she joined with the Ottawa Ex to host an urban music festival. Their partnership began in 1999 and continued for four years. Just as she did with her school's PA system, she eschewed swear words. 'If anyone swore, I would actually unplug their mic,' she says of her efforts to balance the raw energy of rap with a welcoming environment.

Tamara has a knack for garnering media attention and leveraging it when mounting her school tours, which have grown to incorporate funding from a mix of government arts grants and corporate partnerships, with sponsors like the MAC (the cosmetics company) AIDS Fund.

Tamara understands young people, their sophisticated knowledge of pop culture and genuine desire to better understand the world around them. She responds by bringing dedicated and socially aware rap artists like Rochester, Masia One and Eternia into school assemblies. If the kids are rowdy by the end, it's a success. Students stand and chant and laugh and cheer and visibly admire the artists and their deep knowledge of the issues. The question-and-answer period at the end of each assembly is an integral part of the program. Questions around HIV in the developing world or protection and safe sex are the kinds of questions they don't necessarily have the opportunity or gumption to ask in class. (Teachers are asked to continue the debriefing in the classroom immediately following the assembly.) The transformation in the room is palpable, going from a room full of self-conscious adolescents quietly shuffling into a school auditorium to a boisterous collective of energized, engaged young citizens.

Tamara says the 411 is a part of three often distinct worlds. 'On one level, we're part of the arts community,' she says. 'We work with actors, musicians and directors.

'We're also part of the international development community because we work with NGOs on issues that impact young people around the world: human rights, AIDS, children's rights.

'And we're a part of the youth community because we're a youth-led organization,' Tamara says. 'Not all youth organizations we work with do arts and maybe only a third of them do international development work, so it's like there are three circles and we're in the middle, taking a bit from each area.'

Straddling three worlds can make things more difficult, but it also triples the number of potential allies. Partnering is something Tamara recommends as the primary way of getting something off the ground, whether it's a passion project or a career in creating community change. 'From the first shows up until now,' she says, 'something that has made us successful is partnerships. Realize that you can't do it all on your own. You can always do it better if you work with other people, and often there are other people who are doing something with the same theme. You can usually work with them to create a stronger program. The first tour in Ottawa was successful because of college radio and corporate sponsorships, and that was all through networking. And our AIDS program now – every city has an AIDS organization. We partner with them all, which helps us implement the program in every city we visit.'

For the Rebirth Project, Tamara has partnered with music professionals who rep several Toronto community-building groups, including the Remix Project, a City of Toronto–sponsored arts program for at-risk youth. Bryan Brock is a thirty-year-old graphic designer and blogger who teaches graphic design to participants in the Remix Project as head of their Creative Arts program. Andrew Franklin, just twenty-three and also known as Pro Logic, is a music producer whose youth belies his professional experience in recording urban music (he learned the ropes early from his music-producer dad). Pro Logic mentored the Brookside students in laying down beats and recording rhymes, while Brock taught them to manipulate photography in Photoshop to create images for the album art.

For the photography session, Tamara brought in Che Kothari, a twenty-six-year-old photographer, community activist and founder of Manifesto Community Projects, a youth arts organization and annual hip-hop festival. After my visit to Brookside and then to Tamara's office, I meet Che in his west-end Toronto office, a creative hive of photography that looks much like Tamara's place, a repurposed warehouse filled with art and young people having meetings.

While giving a workshop at Brookside, Che made a connection with Brendan, the youngest of the five students. Shyer and quieter than anyone else in class, Brendan took a special interest in photography.

'Instead of his focusing on the music, he was interested in photography,' Che explains. 'We weren't allowed to reveal the identities of these young people, so he came up with the idea of shooting silhouettes,' he says, describing the album art. 'Brendan actually shot it. I showed him how to light it and shoot it, and from there it was passed on to Brock, who did the layout.'

Growing up in an Indo-Canadian family in Guelph, Ontario, Che began taking photos for the high school yearbook when he was fifteen. He then started a photography club. When his family planned a vacation to the Caribbean island of Curaçao, he took took the liberty of borrowing the school's SLR camera for the trip.

'I wasn't supposed to do that,' he laughs. He remembers spending the entire vacation with the school camera around his neck; he came back with great documentation of his eye-opening experience of the island's Carnaval celebration. During his vacation, he noticed that no one questioned him as he hopped fences to be in the mix at the Carnaval – not when he had the camera around his neck. It emboldened him to pursue photography, nixing his father's wishes for him to continue in the family shoe-store business and instead moving to Toronto to attend Ryerson University. His love of music, influenced by his older sisters, and his love of photography meshed to become his life's work, which grew to include community-building through youth activism and the arts.

'I've classified myself as a cultural community instigator,' he says of his work, which includes public speaking at Harvard, the UN Habitat Safer Cities conference and the British Council. 'I work with youth, community engagement, activism, event organization and festival production.'

Che's Manifesto was a natural growth of his love of street art and grassroots music festivals. His friends were interested in the same artistic expression while their skills were diverse in range.

'I feel very strongly that culture can play a role in mitigating violence by giving young people an opportunity and teaching them skills,' Che says. 'In 2005, there were huge violence rates in Toronto. It was the Summer of the Gun. 'We thought, "We need to do something about this. We know so many people."'

Che Kothari at Manifesto

Che organized an initial meeting of twenty friends and colleagues. They met at Toronto City Hall. Che recalls an 'energy' in the city at the time. His social network reflected that. Meetings soon bloomed to double the size. Che noticed that his friends were ethnically diverse but that gender parity wasn't strong. He worked to correct that. When they opened meetings to the public, seventy-five people showed. It kept growing.

'We started to invite funders, policy-makers; the Laidlaw Foundation started coming to the meetings. Someone from Red

Bull would come and listen and contribute to the conversation,' he says. 'Groups like Laidlaw and Canadian Heritage were recognizing Manifesto and hip hop as part of a larger movement.'

Che's partnership with Canadian Heritage and Laidlaw helped him down the road when he negotiated with landlords, seeking to rent a space for his growing artist collective. He cites the importance of being able to communicate with potential partners by speaking their language; he can write the kind of reports Heritage needs, for example, but he also connects with young people through videos that showcase Manifesto events and work.

'An eighty-page report is great and it works in certain spheres, but I have this Blackberry and we can be sitting in a park and I can show you a video. That's how young people get a message across,' he says.

By 2007, they were ready to create an annual hip-hop festival and had 150 people at their meetings, sharing stories and eager to make it happen.

In 2009, Manifesto partnered with LIFE Movement (Learning Initiatives Fostering Elevation), a group of youth advocates centred at Jane and Finch. Together, they brought hip-hop legend KRS-One to Toronto where he spoke at an event inside City Hall, sitting in the mayoral seat, no less.

'Six hundred and fifty people came out, young and old,' he says. KRS-One spoke for an hour, describing his Stop the Violence campaign in New York City. Dalton Higgins, a Toronto author and hip-hop expert, moderated the discussion. While KRS-One's celebrity generated buzz, Che emphasized the importance of including Grassroots Youth Collaborative, a local group, in the discussion. They presented a report called 'The Roots of Youth Violence.'

'It was great we had KRS-One in the spot, you know, but we really wanted to connect it to what's going on locally,' says Che.

This year, 2010, marked the fourth incarnation of the Manifesto Festival of Community and Culture, which has grown to become a seven-day event across Toronto, culminating in a free outdoor hip-hop concert at Yonge-Dundas Square.

'There's great work being done,' Che says of community organization in Toronto, citing the Better Ballots effort to effect electoral reform. 'I don't think there's a deficit in leadership or political will or activism. It's happening in so many different ways, but with grassroots stuff, you do have to find allies in the system.'

Che has the same advice about partnering that Tamara does when it comes to building something from the ground up and trying to harness people's energy for change. 'None of the work I have done or ever will do is a solo thing,' he says. 'It's always a community thing. My methodology has been partnership.'

Meeting with Che and Tamara was an eye-opener for me, showing me how individuals of varying personalities can achieve the same goals. While Che bubbles with voluble overtures, Tamara parses few words, but neither is shy – they are both natural leaders, albeit with different styles.

While leadership may be a shape-shifting quality, the bottom line is always the same: to make change, you need money. Not necessarily a lot, but financial support is necessary and getting it isn't always easy. I asked Che and Tamara about the nuts and bolts of accessing grants and corporate sponsorship.

Although Tamara hasn't been successful on every proposal, she's been great at landing grants since high school – enough to keep the 411 in action. She has several tips for those looking to do the same.

'Meet with the program officer in person first to discuss the project,' she says. 'You may have to push hard to get the meeting. With some places, this means nagging, calling a lot and knowing it is their job to meet with you and support you in writing the grant,' she advises.

She also stresses the importance of research. 'Who else did they fund? What were the projects?'

And for those who may not be coming from a world where writing proposals is the norm, she says you need to learn to speak the language: 'Use language that is appropriate to those reading the grant. Define any youth or arts terms that they may not know.'

Lastly, she has one more tip: 'Learn Results-Based Management formats. If you don't know what that is, Google it.'

The internet is an extremely useful tool. Tamara and Che, and their like-minded peers, seek out partnerships through networking, and while there is no magic expressway to connecting with future partners, there is something that comes close: social media. Facebook, Twitter, Foursquare, Yelp and all the online community message boards we develop through participation and pure personal interest are the same tools you can use to engage fellow future partners in community endeavours. With networking, one door leads to another. What's great about social media, even more than its democratic nature for gregarious and shy types alike, is that it allows for hyperlocal news and information, perfect for those who want to create change within their own communities. Social media is key and, in many ways, natural for a younger generation who may already unwittingly practice what Tamara and Che preach – that nothing is possible without collaboration.

Back at Brookside, the 411 mentors and Brookside admin agreed to juggle schedules so that Daniel and Gary could eventually record their songs. A couple of months later, their music was serviced to DJs, packaged as an MP3 and a CD in a jewel case with art, a tactile result of their efforts.

But after the ten-week Rebirth Project is over, the 411 is in a rebuilding phase. Everyone involved feels it was a success, but to repeat the program, Tamara needs to access more money. And the stop-and-start nature of this kind of funding has led her to try to find support outside of grants.

'Because the program is so unique, it's difficult to find funding,' Tamara says. They'll have to provide reports, apply for more money, then wait and see. Tamara hopes to make a version of the program to target female youth in the detention system.

In the meantime, she has begun collaborating with a consultant who works on sustainability issues for NGOs that are funded by the grant system. 'It can be hard when you don't know where your operating budget is going to come from next year,' Tamara says.

While the money is often erratic, her goals are not. 'We have a very specific vision and unique programming, and we really want to focus on doing what we set out to do, like stuff we were doing at Brookside. No one else is offering that type of program. We're a boutique organization in that we don't want to be doing what everyone else is doing. We're looking to continue to find niche areas like that where we can continue to exist.'

As of this writing, Tamara has received enough money to develop a new school tour for girls. She is taking a few months in the fall of 2010 to develop the program, which will encompass the topics of bullying and body issues. In an attempt to maintain financial stability, the 411 will be charging schools a fee for this program.

The tour will begin in March 2011, with twenty dates in Ontario, after which she hopes to make it available outside the province.

In the years since she organized her first high school assembly, she has mounted twelve to fifteen school tours, visiting schools across Canada and providing remote programming with teachers' kits to schools in every single province and territory. She figures the 411 has presented to well over 300,000 students in person, counting all 'bums in seats, whether they were awake or not,' Tamara jokes.

By the fall of 2010, all but one of the five students in the Rebirth Project have moved on from Brookside. Louise Nadeau, the school's VP, still drives around with the CD in her car, playing it for any new passenger who will listen.

The album consists of two songs. 'Who We Are' is honest self-expression with positive lyrics, a song Nadeau finds inspiring: 'No big house, no fancy cars, this is who we are, this is who we are/I'm a shine bright like a shooting star, this is who we are, this is who we are.'

The other song is called 'Close to the Edge.' In it, Daniel has recorded the lines he rapped for me when we met in the interview room at Brookside in the spring.

And I made a lot of choices in life I gotta live with,
Cats wanna stall my life just like stick shift,
So when you stuck in a box it's a real mess,
They'll have you talkin' through the wire like Mr. West,
And yeah, I'm pissed off, I'm close to the edge,
I might jump and fall off the map just like Kris Kross,
So tell me what's going on?

Daniel has the same pissed-off energy that motivated Tamara at his age, the same energy that led her to create the 411 Initiative for Change. If he's reading this, wherever he may be today, he should know that anger, like Tamara's, can be channelled to create change. If you need a road map, many exist, including Tamara's and Che's. The way to get there is to partner with others going in a similar direction.

Get involved

whatsthe411.ca

themanifesto.ca

myspace.com/thelifemovementtdot

Hannah Sung is a columnist with the *Globe and Mail* and *Flare* magazine. She worked with the 411 Initiative for Change as a host in 2008, presenting in Canadian high schools on the topic of HIV/AIDS. She is currently a Fellow at the Writers' Institute at the Graduate Center of City University of New York.

Christina Palassio
Taking a Schein to City Hall
A community activist runs for Council in Ward 17

Jonah Schein spent election night in the wood-panelled ballroom of the Hungarian House, a community centre and banquet hall on St. Clair Avenue West. The party, thrown in honour of Ward 21 incumbent Joe Mihevc, school trustee candidate Adam Chaleff-Freudenthaler and Schein, a candidate for councillor in Ward 17, was billed as a victory celebration for all three candidates. As a few Schein campaign volunteers and I made our way to the Hungarian House from the phone bank on Westmount Avenue, Schein was ahead in the polls where some of us had been scrutineers, and the mood was cautiously optimistic. Everyone had doubts about Schein's chances, but recent endorsements from the *Toronto Star*, ArtsVote, *Eye Weekly*, the Toronto Environmental Alliance, *NOW*, *Torontoist* and the Public Transit Coalition, along with media reports of high voter turnout, had buoyed hopes. At 8:10 on October 25, 2010, we walked into the ballroom, and into Mayor Rob Ford's Toronto. A few minutes later, Citytv declared the incumbent councillor, Cesar Palacio, the winner in Ward 17. (The final vote count would be 6,154 for Palacio and 4,827 for Schein.) Dozens of Schein's friends and volunteer supporters, many of whom had come straight from phone banks, polling booths and final pull-the-vote canvass rounds, stood sombrely around small television sets, unable to unglue their eyes from the screens. After a few half-hearted conversations, a bunch of us fled the bad news for the front steps of the building, chased by waves of lamenting *what-nows*.

The story of Schein's campaign is a variation on countless election narratives: candidates spend months walking up and down streets, often at considerable personal sacrifice, to talk with people about the ways in which their neighbourhoods could be better.

Descriptions of a city under siege abounded in the months leading up to Toronto's 2010 municipal election, yet few people seemed to make the connection that a change at City Hall could happen only if people across the city – activists, business owners, community leaders, etc. – put themselves forward as alternatives to the status quo. No matter how imperfect the process and disappointing the potential for loss, someone has to step up and take responsibility for bringing under-represented voices to the fore. While there are many good reasons to be cynical about the idea of public service as effective activism, the fact remains that to build a good city, the people who fight for the Toronto they want need good city councillors who will listen to their needs and ideas.

Until July 2010, Schein was the Civic Engagement Coordinator at the Stop Community Food Centre, where he helped residents in the organization's catchment area gain increased access to healthy food, settlement assistance, welfare support and housing advice. (Disclosure moment: I started working at the Stop two weeks before Schein left.) Schein is a broad-shouldered, engaging thirty-six-year-old anti-poverty activist, the eldest of four siblings who grew up in the School House, an alternative school on St. Clair Avenue West run by their parents. A few years ago, Schein returned to live in Ward 17 with his partner, Velvet, a teacher. Over his five years with the Stop, Schein, who has a master's in social work from York University witnessed how the area's inhabitants were being left out, bot within their own ward and in the greater municipal convers tion. Davenport West is characterized by significant pockets poverty concentrated along the Davenport and Lansdowne the Vaughan and Oakwood axes; residents in those neighb hoods struggle to make ends meet on paltry wages and in cient levels of social assistance. Much of Schein's wor aimed at giving these residents the tools and confide share their experiences in forums where they would otherwise go unnoticed. In his time at the Stop, Schein co-organized several community action campaigns, most visible among them the 2010 Do the Math campaign, in which several high-profile Torontonians – among them Mihevc, Damian Abraham from the band Fucked Up and writer Naomi Klein – took up the challenge to live for as long as possible on a food-bank hamper to raise awareness about atrophying levels of welfare support in the province.

One night in early June, Schein's younger brother Anthony, special assistant to Mihevc, the councillor in the next ward, came to his house to ask if he would challenge incumbent Cesar Palacio for the ward's Council seat. 'I wasn't expecting him to take it is seriously,' the energetic twenty-six-year-old remembers. When his brother agreed to think about it, the younger Schein began harnessing support. 'Jonah had told me not to tell anyone but I went ahead and told Joe, who got excited right away, and Alejandra [Bravo], and tried to build pressure on him from them.' Bravo was the reason Anthony had come to see his brother in the first place; the quintilingual mother of three had run against Palacio in the previous two elections, losing by only 281 votes in 2006. Now a manager at the Maytree Foundation, she had opted not to run in the 2010 election. Mihevc and community organizers in Ward 17 were looking for someone familiar with the issues facing the community to take up the charge.

Without any real political experience, Schein wondered what could possibly qualify him to be a city councillor, but his experiences advocating on behalf of the under-represented in the ward compelled him to consider his brother's proposal. On July 1, Schein emailed Anthony and told him he'd run. He paints his decision as mostly altruistic: 'I thought, it's so unfortunate that Bravo did this work for two races, that she built up the support in the community and the infrastructure that's necessary for a

Jonah Schein, right, with brother Anthony

campaign, and that all that would go to waste if nobody picked up the ball this time. So I started thinking about it, just to keep things alive in this neighbourhood and to support what I hoped would be a movement of socially minded people at different levels of government.'

Both Schein brothers took leaves of absence from their jobs, rented a storefront on St. Clair at Alberta Avenue, and started rounding up friends and family to volunteer. Neither had run a campaign before. Anthony, the campaign's newly minted chair, looked to Bravo's former campaign manager, Sean Hill, veteran political organizer Ann Decter, Mihevc and Bravo herself for support and advice. Help also came from Schein's former co-workers and the many community members he'd worked with in his five years at the Stop. Schein got some public-relations help from a friend, actor Greg Landucci, and planned a campaign launch party at the Hungarian House on August 26. He rounded up almost 200 volunteers and raised $15,000 that night; his speech, however, was anticlimactic: 'Wow. Uh, hey,' he started. He continued, with a trembling voice and shaking hands, to decry the conditions in the ward's public housing and the general feeling of disengagement he saw in certain communities. While the points in his speech were compelling, Schein's tendency to mumble made it difficult to hear what he was saying. Anyone from an opposing camp would have been reassured by his performance.

Ward 17 is shaped like a bottle, and sprawls between Eglinton Avenue, Oakwood Avenue, Dupont Street and Old Weston Road. It has long been a Portuguese and Italian enclave, but has recently seen an influx of Vietnamese, Jamaican and East Indian residents, as well as couples and young families who can't afford homes in the rapidly gentrifying Bloorcourt neighbourhood to the south. Cesar Palacio, Toronto's first Hispanic councillor, has represented the ward for more than two decades, first as an assistant to Betty Disero, the area's pre-amalgamation councillor, and then as a councillor himself. Palacio's support base is strong, especially among the area's long-time Portuguese and Italian residents, but Schein felt a change in representation was needed.

In his attempt to unseat Palacio, Schein was banking on the votes of former Bravo supporters, as well as the ward's new residents. He chose to build his campaign on a believers' platform of civic engagement, focusing on free transit for students and seniors; a citywide bedbug policy; halting the diesel-fuelled Union Station–Pearson Airport rail link; support of small businesses, especially those that had been laid flat by the construction of the St. Clair streetcar right-of-way; more parks and green spaces; and tenants' rights. The St. Clair right-of-way became a key issue during the campaign, further dividing an already polarized Schein (for) and Palacio (very much against). Throughout it all, Schein's main argument – most vociferously expressed at an all-candidates debate held at Oakwood Collegiate Institute that was plagued by Palacio's negative rhetoric and attended by dozens of disgruntled hecklers – was that a councillor should build a city, not fight it.

In a municipal race dominated by talk of cutting taxes and slashing spending, communicating the importance of community gardens in a couple of minutes on someone's doorstep is even harder than it sounds. But as Schein's campaign gained momentum, so did his sense of urgency. With every new conversation, the subtext was that Ward 17 was running out of time. The Gem, previously just a good place for beer and nachos on Davenport near Ossington, became the unofficial campaign headquarters. Schein could often be found there after canvassing rounds, speaking in his distinctive low and fast mumble about tenants' rights, lawn-sign strategies and optimal campaign foods. Schein had endorsements from Mihevc and Bravo, and quickly got the support of budget chief Shelley Carroll, councillors Gord Perks and Adam Vaughan, and labour and tenants' associations. He traded in his jeans and T-shirts for dress pants and a beige trench coat. One of his friends remarked, with a mixture of surprise and awe, how strange it was that his new campaign volunteers seemed to know a different Schein than the unpolished, off-the-cuff activist that she knew. As he became more practiced at the two-minute pitch and the calibrated response, Schein's message stayed the same: more parks, better access to childcare, more community events where people could come out of their houses and talk to each other.

Defeating an incumbent is tough. Municipal campaigns are long, drawn-out affairs, much longer than provincial or federal campaigns. Many people are tired, worn out, too busy or too indifferent to pay attention. When you have little to no name recognition, knocking on doors all day can be an exercise in ego destruction.

Some days are good: early in his campaign, canvassing up a side street, Schein met a man who was so frustrated with the stasis in the ward that he wrote Schein's campaign a cheque within five minutes of meeting him. Schein was so taken aback he had to call

So, you want to run for City Council? Here are 21 easy steps to help you get your 2014 campaign started.

1. Get angry about what's going on in your ward and start talking to people about it.
2. Get a campaign team together. Does your friend draw maps? Maybe she wants to help you with your canvassing plans. Is your sister always talking money? Get her to helm your fundraising team!
3. Get the endorsement of high-visibility supporters in the ward. Business owners, community leaders, well-connected moms, long-time residents: leave no phone uncalled.
4. By this point, you've already enlisted your family, friends, co-workers to volunteer for your campaign. Now put out the call to acquaintances and strangers. University students on summer break are good. So are people who spend too much time on Twitter complaining about the way things are.
5. Register as a candidate. It only costs $100. Registration usually opens ten months prior to election day. Check the City of Toronto Elections website for updates on candidates' info sessions.
6. Throw a campaign launch/fundraiser, and make sure no one leaves before they've committed time or money (or both) to your campaign. Tell them about your website, where you've posted your platform, the address of your campaign office and any endorsements you've already received.
7. Brief your volunteers on your platform and organize canvasser training sessions.
8. As early as possible, start knocking on doors. If you know you're heading into a neighbourhood where many people speak Portuguese, bring your Portuguese-speaking friends to help facilitate conversation.
9. Identify interest groups who represent the issues in your platform – labour unions, organizations like ArtsVote and the Toronto

Environmental Alliance, tenants' and ratepayers' associations, etc. – and make sure they know about you.

10. Participate in all-candidates debates; bring supporters, not hecklers.

11. Get endorsements from councillors who share your vision of the city, and let the media know when you get them.

12. Make sure your fridge is stocked with sandwiches. (Better yet, take a page from Ward 19 candidate Karen Sun's campaign and encourage friends and volunteers to organize a cooking group that'll whip up tasty meals you can scarf down between canvass rounds.)

13. Keep hoofing it.

14. Keep fundraising, even if you've already reached your goal. There are sure to be unexpected costs down the line.

15. More debates.

16. Get your director of marketing to prepare election literature in as many languages as possible. In your downtime, make sure you create an attention-grabbing social media campaign – see the spoof 'Schein for Davenport' videos on YouTube – that can help get people talking about you.

17. While on chocolate-covered-espresso-bean highs, plan your campaign-literature drops.

18. Set a lawn-sign goal and meet it. (One thousand is a nice round number to start with.) Gather your friends for a midnight sign run the day they can go up. (Not before!)

19. Knock on more doors. Don't bother visiting supporters and non-supporters twice: spend the last few weeks of your campaign convincing undecideds to come to the polls.

20. Round up a huge crew of volunteers for last-minute pull-the-vote and poll-information call blitz on election day.

21. Plan a celebration party for election night. Whether you win or not, you should celebrate the efforts you and your team have put in over the last few months.

his brother to confirm who the cheque should be made out to. Other days are not so good: a few weeks later, he canvassed up Lansdowne Avenue and met a pyjama-clad woman in her mid-thirties who was unsure if she would vote in the election. She'd lived in the ward for years, but hadn't voted in as long as she could remember and didn't think this race would be the one to drive her to the polls. It was almost 9 p.m., right around the time when a stranger knocking at the door goes from being an imposition to an intrusion. This was Schein's third canvassing round of the day. The woman was decisively indecisive, but Schein didn't let up, barrelling on past the point where he usually said good night. After several minutes of monologuing, seeing that his words were having no visible effect, he exploded: 'You need to vote because I need to open a community office so I can help all these other people who need help!' It didn't matter, he said, whether she planned to live there for another day or another decade: it was her responsibility towards other residents of the ward to vote. 'I'm not trying to be pushy,' he quickly added. 'But you are being pushy,' the woman replied, unfazed. After a short standoff, Schein thanked her for her time and she shut the door. Later, Schein apologized for his outburst. His frustration at the woman's refusal to engage with him made me think of something he'd said a few days after his campaign launch, when we'd sat down in his kitchen to talk about his plans for the coming months. I'd wondered what made him think he could do more for the community within the confines of City Council than as a community activist. His answer was new ears. 'When people say, "We need a speed bump," what they really mean is "We don't want a highway." I want to make sure that stuff is being said.' More important, Schein wanted to make sure someone was there to listen. He saw engaging in the process of municipal politics as a direct form of civic engagement, one that, instead of standing in opposition to the work he'd been doing, might allow him to do that work better.

By the time Schein's campaign neared its close, his more than 400 volunteers had put up 2,000 lawn signs, knocked on thousands of doors and made thousands more phone calls. In his email to supporters on election day, he included a quote by Martin Luther King that his brother kept above his desk: 'The arc of history is long, but it bends toward justice.' 'It is a reminder that our work to improve our neighbourhoods and the larger world around us is a long-term project,' he wrote. 'Despite many setbacks, and many moments where our task feels impossible, we make progress, day by day.' It's idealistic, yes, and in this context even a bit trite. But in an election characterized by angry, negative rhetoric, getting out to hear people's messages with the goal of feeding them back into the community is where Schein and many of the councillor candidates played their most valuable roles. Helping strangers realize that they have agency in their parks, neighbourhoods and schools every day, not just at election time, is their lasting legacy. In three months, Schein went from being a stranger to many residents in the ward to getting 33 per cent of the more than 14,000 votes cast. He lost, but at the election-night party, he read the victory speech he'd worked on with his sister until 2 a.m. Strangely, it didn't sound out of place.

Get involved

electjonahschein.com
dothemath.thestop.org
putfoodinthebudget.ca

Christina Palassio is the co-editor of several books in the *uTOpia* series, including *HtO: Toronto's Water from Lake Iroquois to Lost Rivers to Low-flow Toilets* and *The Edible City: Toronto's Food from Farm to Fork*. She has also written for the *Globe and Mail*, the Montreal *Gazette* and *Matrix* magazine, and is the books columnist for *THIS Magazine*.

Jennifer Lewington
The media and your message

Tucked behind the sprawling Eglinton Flats at Jane Street in northwest Toronto is the community of Mount Dennis, one of thirteen 'priority neighbourhoods' identified by the City for their high incidence of poor newcomers and inadequate urban services.

Eglinton Flats Park straddles Jane Street and Eglinton Avenue and, for some Mount Dennis residents, it once epitomized the deteriorating state of their community. A ravine that slopes down on the south side of the park had, in 2004, become a dumping ground for mattresses, shopping carts and other garbage. No one felt comfortable walking at night around the natural pond in the park.

'There was a feeling of neglect in the community,' recalls resident Jean Boutot. Local residents, she added, felt that 'civic leaders were not paying attention to anyone [in Mount Dennis].'

Neither were the media.

Save for the occasional shooting, Mount Dennis draw little media attention, especially from the Toronto City Hall Press Gallery, which operates in its own clubby yet competitive world on the ground floor of the 'clam shell' at 100 Queen Street West. Reporters from the mainstream media – the *Globe and Mail*, the *Toronto Star*, the *Toronto Sun*, Toronto Community News, CBC, CTV, private radio stations and so on – work in busy satellite bureaus filing stories on a wide range of civic issues. The rhythm of news is marked by monthly committee and Council meetings, informal media 'scrums' afterwards and, on other occasions, sporadic press conferences by politicians and interest groups. The daily drumbeat, intensified by the twenty-four-hour-a-day demands of the internet, leaves little chance for a City Hall reporter to break free of deadline constraints to carry out research on a story unless it is sure to make the six o'clock news.

Jean Boutot

But out of media sight, something was afoot in Mount Dennis. In the fall of 2004, Boutot and her neighbours talked to each other and put together a to-do list, starting with a cleanup of the park. The following spring, as snow melted to reveal a season's worth (or more) of litter on Toronto streets, Citytv started to prepare a feature on the dirtiest areas of the city. Boutot remembers receiving a phone call from a friend who had seen the segment, which listed Jane and Eglinton as the third-dirtiest neighbourhood in Toronto.

Proud of the cleanup activities already on the go in her community, Boutot fired off an email to Citytv about the work of volunteers known as the Dirty Dozen. 'Anytime you want to see a real cleanup crew in action, come out this spring. We are ready to go,' she wrote. 'We are sick and tired of waiting for the City to do it.'

To her astonishment, Citytv promptly phoned back and whisked Boutot off to Eglinton Flats Park for an interview. A few days later, Citytv returned for a follow-up feature on the neighbourhood's can-do spirit.

'I thought "Wow, what just happened here?"' recalls Boutot, who hid out at home that weekend, embarrassed by the media hoopla. 'In this neighbourhood, we think we are the last ones on the list, and then we realized that others were not doing what we were doing.'

After that initial flurry of publicity, reporters (including some at City Hall) from the *Globe and Mail*, the *Toronto Star* and other news outlets wrote their own stories about Mount Dennis, further raising its profile.

What made Boutot and the Dirty Dozen a surprise hit with the media? They had no media training, knew no reporters at City Hall and issued no press releases to trumpet their work. However, they had the one thing every reporter needs: a compelling story. The volunteer effort in Mount Dennis was about people working together, out of the limelight, to improve their community. They also had an engaging spokeswoman, strong visuals (garbage strewn in the park and ravine) and a bit of the David-and-Goliath dynamic that is beloved by the media. Last but not least, they had the serendipity of timing – Citytv's immediate need for local examples for its feature on dirty streets and parks in Toronto.

Connecting with the media is rarely as simple as firing off an email. But what happened in Mount Dennis demonstrates the power of the media when it chooses to put the spotlight on a community group or an activist cause. What distinguished the Dirty Dozen from others who toil in anonymity was the presence of a strong narrative – a storyline, or a hook, as it's known in journalism. Without it, reporters can't do their job, which is to grapple, every day, with the same question: What's happening?

At City Hall, the answer to that question flows from steady streams of information: public reports from bureaucrats, reaction from councillors and the mayor, and the lobbyists and special interests all vying to control the political agenda. Too often missing from the City Hall story is the voice of residents and community groups whose opinions and anecdotes bring a news story to life.

In other words, a marriage of interest exists between the reporter and the activist/community group. What does it take to develop that relationship? Planning and practice to hone 'the pitch.' Long before they phone a reporter or assignment editor, activists need to think about the identity of their own organization and why the public ought to hear about its work.

Catching the ear or eye of a reporter is only a first step in the process. Just as reporters receive a pitch for a story, they in turn must propose it to an editor, who in turn must persuade colleagues of the merits of the story. With shrinking news holes at newspapers, shorter time for broadcasts and competition from new media on the internet, only certain stories get top billing. Others, even deserving ones, may not see the light of day. There is no single formula for making a winning pitch to the media, but there are some necessary ingredients without which success will be elusive.

Know what makes news

From the moment a community group tries to seek publicity for its cause to the final decision by news editors to pursue the story (or not), two questions dominate the conversation: 'Why now?' and 'Who cares?' The reporter will put these questions to a community group and will have to answer them when they're posed by an editor. Given the intense competition from other stories vying for scarce space in the newspaper or time on the news broadcast, the two questions serve as a filtering device.

A story with no time element falls to the bottom of the heap; another one gets attention because something interesting, funny or dramatic is happening to someone and the public needs to know now. A positive answer to 'Why now?' and 'Who cares?' means there is a storyline about someone doing something or having something (good or bad) done to them that should matter to the rest of us at this moment.

Even before they approach the media, activists and community groups should ask themselves those two questions and develop a response akin to an 'elevator pitch' that's no more than thirty seconds long. To an editor or reporter, the word 'Boring!' is the ultimate insult for a story that lacks immediacy, relevance or colour.

'If you have a good answer [to the two questions], then you probably have a good story,' says David Israelson, a former newspaper reporter, editorial writer and foreign correspondent for the *Toronto Star* who spent eleven years as a vice-president and editor at Toronto-based Media Profile, a public affairs and government relations firm. As a journalist, he reported on local citizens who took the lead on recycling efforts ahead of elected officials. As a public affairs advisor, he now coaches companies and non-profits on how to get their message out and use the media to influence decisions at City Hall and other levels of government.

Individuals or groups often mistakenly believe their own problem is of interest to others. Not so, he says. 'Often there is special pleading: "You have to do something about a leaking fire hydrant on my lawn,"' he observes. 'That's not interesting.' But the same story could wind up on page one if it exposes a problem with the city's water mains. 'That's different,' says Israelson. 'It leads to a story about how much money we are losing as taxpayers ... and why isn't anyone doing anything about it.'

Other stories involve conflicts between two or more parties – say, a homeowner's annoyance over what she views as weeds in a neighbour's 'natural garden.' That local squabble may not resonate, but takes on immediate significance to the media when the City conducts a crackdown on untidy residential properties. The bottom line for activists, says Israelson, is to 'extrapolate your issue into something that is not just about you, but about other people.'

Know and cultivate the media

Journalists come in all shapes and sizes: the 'gotcha' newshound, the thoughtful reporter, the naturally curious editor and the intellectually lazy columnist are all part of the fabric of journalism. Sorting out who's who is critical for activists. Pay attention to newspaper stories and broadcasts to figure out who takes time to check sources and provide insight despite the constraints of time and space. Recognizing differences among journalists, their attitudes and work ethic could save frustration later.

No matter the quality of the reporter, columnist or assignment editor, they are not advocates, friends or publicity agents. Their job is to explain what happened and why it matters to the public, and to do so in as engaging a way as possible. That's why storytelling is central to the work of a journalist, and why local groups have so much to offer in bringing a story to life.

Before calling reporters or assignment editors, put yourself in their shoes. Does their news organization have any history of covering the kind of story you want to pitch? A hand-wringing tale of a low-income family's lack of access to affordable housing will likely be covered by the *Toronto Star*, but not by the *Globe and Mail*. But the *Globe* might use that same family to highlight a policy change in the provincial budget. In short, read the papers, listen to newscasts and seek out back issues online at the library to develop a profile of a news organization and its interests.

Talk to other activist groups to tap their experience with the media, such as getting a line on a reporter's reputation for fairness and accuracy. Understand, too, the different mandates of journalists. At City Hall, reporters have the luxury of specializing in the civic affairs beat, which enables them to delve into a subject and appreciate the nuances. A general assignment reporter, by contrast, is thrown into a story with little preparation or background. They have to be smart enough just to catch its nub, not every nuance. Still, whether they have a beat or work general assignment, reporters are expected to marshal the facts in an unbiased fashion.

Not so for the columnist, who is paid to have a point of view – one that may run counter to a group's interest. Figure out if a columnist is likely to be sympathetic or, if she is opposed, whether she might be open to rethinking a position based on additional facts.

Those who learn to cultivate relationships with journalists have a better chance of generating public interest in their cause. 'If you are not on the media radar you are not on the radar at all,' warns Cindy Wilkey, chair of the citizen-led West Don Lands Committee, who has dealt with the media on Toronto waterfront renewal for the past decade. Over time, she has developed some basic rules of engagement. 'You've got to be prepared to give good candid background and information,' she says. 'You might say, "I will tell you this but I can't be quoted."'

As well, she emphasizes, assume everything is on the record unless you have an agreement that was made with the journalist before, not after, the interview. 'When you are not used to dealing with the media, sometimes people are surprised about what will get reported,' she says. 'If you say something outrageous or catchy, they will want to put that down.'

Above all, she adds, practice what you want to say before opening your mouth. Before she speaks to a journalist, Wilkey writes out her main points and refers to them in the interview, ensuring she sticks to her message.

Have a game plan

In late 2005, the Royal Ontario Museum sparked outrage in its Annex neighbours and the University of Toronto when it proposed an ambitious plan to build a forty-six-storey condo on the site of the former McLaughlin Planetarium. To proceed, the ROM would need planning permission to rezone a cultural district for residential use.

Members of the Annex Residents' Association, a group that was instrumental in the 1960s defeat of the Spadina Expressway, realized they had to mobilize quickly to defeat the ROM project. They also knew that residents opposed to a new development, especially a high-rise tower on a subway corridor, run the risk of being dismissed by the media as 'not-in-my-backyard' naysayers. The Annex residents wanted to send a more positive, sophisticated message: no to this project, but yes to thoughtful city planning.

Long-time Annex residents Sandra Shaul and Mimi Fuller- ton, members of the ARA, helped lead the campaign that ulti- mately forced the ROM to withdraw its widely criticized project. 'It's like a political campaign, where you have to create your message and stay on message,' says Shaul.

The residents' association made a point of reaching out to similar groups across the city, a strategy that led to more than 350 citizens showing up to a community meeting in November 2005 to voice almost universal opposition to the tower. The message that was delivered through the media was that the ROM tower proposal had implications for other neighbour- hoods in Toronto. 'This was not just an Annex issue,' Shaul told the *Town Crier* in December 2005. 'We are just closest to it. This is bigger than the Annex.'

A disciplined game plan requires an articulate spokesperson (and a backup ally) who can keep the message simple, and meaningful to the public. 'What happens sometimes in neigh- bourhood fights is that people have all the right reasons for their fight but the communications and the strategy are garbled,' observes Fullerton. 'You have to be disciplined on both.'

Sticking to the message is essential. Shaul recalls one interview in which a CBC radio reporter tried to frame another development dispute, a proposed high-rise condo at One Bedford Avenue, as a simple game of winners and losers. She refused to get boxed in and stuck with the ARA message that local residents play a vital role in good city planning. The high-rise project went ahead, with some modifications. But the residents won a major victory by spurring a City-sponsored local advisory committee made up of community and business stakeholders that was tasked with establishing principles to guide the future development of Bloor Street between Avenue Road and Bathurst Street. The Bloor Corridor Visioning Study addressed issues of streetscape improvements, pedestrian safety, heritage and infrastructure and, more broadly, served as a model for an informed conversation between neighbourhood groups and developers.

Recognize the impact of timing

The seismic shift rocking professional journalism – the rise of the twenty-four-hour news cycle, online newspapers, free subway papers and the emergence of social media outlets such as Twitter – has redefined what, when, how (and by whom) news is delivered. A decade ago, a City Hall reporter might write one story every day or two and put together a feature for the weekend. Now that same reporter begins the day with a quick feed to the online version of the newspaper from a press conference by the mayor. Then it's time to fire off a gossipy item to the paper's online City Hall blog. Meanwhile, an editor calls with a request to file quotes to another reporter. Given the intensifying competitive pressure of the new business, the reporter is now expected to make full use of social-media tools like Twitter to post a message and flag the online story. By late afternoon, it's finally time to write for tomorrow's paper, hopefully with more context and details than the online story that appeared earlier in the day.

The go-go-go atmosphere leaves less and less time for a deadline-driven reporter to think about or seek out community groups. So make it easy for the reporter and recognize that timing matters. For example, if a report on a controversial development will be before committee in a week or so, contact the reporter ahead of time and ask if she plans to cover the presentation, and if she'd be interested in talking to some real people. With the right ingredients – people, conflict and why the story matters to others – a reporter can put together a story for Monday's paper, the slowest of the week, before the committee meeting. The news coverage could influence the outcome of the debate.

In early 2008, John O'Keefe was walking home from his favourite pub late one night when he was struck down on Yonge Street by a bullet intended for someone else. In the wake of the senseless death, the grieving friends of the forty-two-year-old father quickly put together a Facebook page in his memory. The speed with which they moved to develop the site and their readiness to share photos of him with the print and broadcast outlets guaranteed a human face was put on the tragedy.

Timing is a valuable tool in everyday situations, too. Keep a calendar tied to the monthly cycle of committee reports and Council meetings at City Hall. Reporters are more likely to pay attention to an issue when it's about to bubble up as a political conflict at Council. Look for other links to activities that coincide with decisions coming to Council, making it to easy to answer the questions 'Why now?' and 'Who cares?'

Make use of well-placed people

In 1999, the citizen-led West Don Lands Committee held a three-day forum on the future of Toronto's waterfront. The event coincided with a pledge by Ottawa, the province and Toronto to invest in waterfront renewal for the city's 2008 Olympic bid.

Given the spike in political attention to the waterfront, the West Don Lands Committee invited local residents, design experts and leading urban thinkers to the three-day workshop. 'We wanted to make sure we had the right spin on it [to get mainstream media] attention,' recalls Wilkey of the West Don Lands Committee. One of the top names at the event was Joan Busquets, the renowned urban planner and architect who played a key role in Barcelona's 1992 Olympic Games.

The Toronto forum wrapped up with scenarios for waterfront renewal presented by three design teams. There was only one problem: the event wound up on a Saturday afternoon, the deadest time of the week for media coverage. Moreover, there was no 'hard news' from the forum, whose goal was to produce conceptual ideas about waterfront renewal.

'We had to find a hook ... and we had to make it easy for the media,' recalls Wilkey. The hook was a press conference at City Hall on the following Monday morning. Reporters showed up to hear a spirited call to arms for waterfront renewal from Mr. Busquets and Toronto's then chief city planner, Paul Bedford. 'We got a pretty big draw,' Wilkey recalled with amazement. 'It was our biggest splash where we intentionally went out to get a bunch of media.'

Done right, a press conference is a simple and convenient way to get out a message. Drop by the main-floor press gallery at City Hall and speak to whoever is the president (a working journalist elected by his or her peers). In that conversation, you can work out when it will be a good time (given the competing demands on a reporter's schedule) to show up with a spokesperson, handouts and visual material to tell the story. If there's a lot going on, the gallery president may make it clear that a press conference may not make sense at that moment. Alternatively, it might be just the right time for reporters to do a little one-stop shopping with a group that can bring life to an issue.

Another option is to show up at the press gallery and drop off a press release in the mailboxes set aside for news organizations. Reporters constantly check for what's being dropped off by City officials and interest groups and, if there's an issue of interest, they'll follow up with the contacts on the press release.

Look beyond the mainstream media

Not every deserving story earns coverage in the mainstream media. That's less of an issue these days because there are so many ways to get out a story using social-media sites such as Facebook, Twitter, YouTube and blogs.

The traditional media used to be the sole gatekeepers of news. No more. Much to the annoyance of the White House press corps, who stand at the top of the journalistic heap in the United States, President Barack Obama's press secretary, Robert Gibbs, has no qualms about sending out breaking news on Twitter. The same strategy played out at City Hall earlier this year when Mayor David Miller and City bureaucrats announced he would hold a press conference the next day but refused to divulge the topic. In the absence of information, some City Hall reporters (and their editors) speculated wildly that Miller would jump into the mayoral race or announce he was heading to the United Nations for an environmental job. The truth was the mayor wanted to announce on live

Top ten tips for pitching a story to the media

• What's your story? In thirty seconds or less, answer, 'Why now?' and 'Who cares?'

• Make it easy: don't assume a reporter knows your issue. Put relevant facts on one page, including contacts for daytime, after-hours and email.

• Make friends. Enlist other organizations that may have more experience in dealing with reporters. Seek out unlikely allies who can attract media interest.

• Develop a website and use Facebook and Twitter to spread the word. A cleverly designed website or social-media campaign may spark interest from reporters who know nothing about your cause.

• Don't be afraid to pick up the phone: reporters need your stories to give a human dimension to an issue or debate.

• Have a game plan. Define the core message, figure out the reason for going public and identify the desired outcomes.

• Practice your message. Keep it simple.

• Identify key spokespersons who will stay on message.

• Don't whine and don't fake it. Reporters have a nose for self-serving antics.

• Share the load. Take advantage of the skills of your own group, recognizing that the youngest members have much to offer.

television – unfiltered by the media – an unexpected budget surplus that would take the sting out of a proposed property tax increase for 2010.

Councillor Joe Mihevc (St. Paul's) is a keen proponent of using social media to get out the word to his constituents. When the City rolled out its new fleet of garbage bins, he created a YouTube video with fellow councillor Glenn De Baeremaeker, chair of the city works committee, to demonstrate the do's and don'ts of recycling in Toronto.

Like the mayor and councillors, local groups can reach over the heads of the traditional press to get out a message using a smart website or social-media campaign to highlight their activities and accomplishments. A clear, concise message, told in a clever way, can win new friends and allies and, in the process, catch the eye of an enterprising reporter.

Putting it all together

Local activist Desmond Cole first came to media attention as a finalist in the 2006 City Idol competition, an inventive campaign designed to encourage a new generation, including young, black residents like Cole, to get involved in the municipal election that year.

Four years later, Cole is now the project coordinator for I Vote Toronto, an advocacy group campaigning to give landed immigrants the right to vote in local elections before they become Canadians. It's not an easy sell: there's no obvious crisis, and no pressing deadline for the province to change its rules. So why put in a big lobbying effort for the October 25 municipal election in Toronto? Simple: the media is paying attention.

'The more exposure people have to this idea ... the more they feel comfortable getting behind it,' says Cole, recognizing the media's power to shape public opinion. His goal is to secure commitments for election reform from as many mayoral and

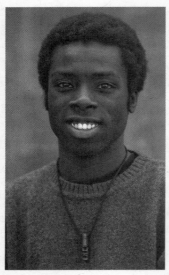

Desmond Cole

Council candidates as possible, making it hard for the province to ignore the issue.

The lessons he's learned from past dealings with the media are shaping his election-reform strategy. One is the importance of developing relationships. Through the Maytree Foundation, a major sponsor of the extend-the-vote campaign, Cole met a producer with TV Ontario and exchanged business cards. He kept in touch and, months later, as the voting issue picked up steam, he received a call to appear on TVO's current-affairs program *The Agenda*.

Another lesson is the value of working with allies. In May 2010, Cole moderated a mayoral debate sponsored by Better Ballots, a grassroots initiative to make local democracy more accessible. That night, six of eight candidates for mayor endorsed extending the local vote to newcomers. I Vote Toronto also worked with like-minded candidates for Council and community groups doing their own outreach for the election to identify residents who, though ineligible to vote, added their voice to calls for change.

'You need to find allies – policy allies – who are doing the same thing,' says Cole. It's part of his strategy to build momentum and attract media attention. After a *Toronto Star* columnist endorsed the idea and *Eye Weekly* ran a favourable spread, others joined in with an opposing view. That stirred controversy and more media attention. 'We got phone calls from radio and TV,' says Cole. 'The media stuff comes in waves.'

Given the power of community groups to lead civic change, the last word goes to Jean Boutot. 'You are the authority,' she advises activists working to improve the quality of life in their city. 'If you are living it [your issue], breathing it, you are there and you are the resident expert.' That's when it's time to tell your story to the media.

Get involved

peopleplantoronto.org
theara.org
ivotetoronto.org

Jennifer Lewington is an award-winning freelance journalist who writes on urban affairs and education issues for newspapers and magazines in Canada and the U.S. In 2010, she wrapped up a twenty-nine-year career with the *Globe and Mail*, where she was named the paper's first female foreign correspondent in 1984 and wrote on local, national and international issues from Ottawa, Washington, D.C., and Toronto. She was a co-winner of a National Newspaper Award for her coverage of free trade in the late 1980s and was named a Nieman Fellow at Harvard University for 1990–91. She and her husband, George Pearson, live in Stratford, Ontario.

Mike Smith
'Exhilarated and heartbroken'
Dispatches from a creative city still to come

Ours is a creative city. Rife with 'creative sectors' and 'creative industries,' employing 'creative workers' from the 'Creative Class,' we Torontonians barrel forth in a creative lather to emerge as leaders in the new 'creative economy.' (Immune, we hope, to the sorts of creative math recently seen to be working at the core of the old economy.)

A small fleet of architectural flagships, more (and more visible) festivals and a couple of new high-rent hives for the consultant caste continually imply an approaching groundswell of Creativity – though often all there is to report from ground level is a swelling rank of folks willing to embrace 'freelancer' as the new 'unemployed.'

The term 'Creative Class' poses an interesting contradiction: both permissive and proscriptive, an open exhortation to the artistic spirit and a delineation of where it resides. There's Creative This-and-That, and there's everything else.

Not even the most hermetic novelist works in a vacuum: to seek a creative city is really to seek a city of collaboration. And collaboration only occurs, by definition, between equals. And so, self-styled prophets of 'creativity,' as a strategy for civic renewal, cut complicated figures. Depending on your vantage, they could be prophets of egalitarian post-Fordist creativity or harbingers of a redux post-industrial inequality.

'Everyone is creative,' wrote Richard Florida, in his watershed book whose title, *The Rise of the Creative Class*, suggested precisely otherwise – placing 'creativity' into a profound state of tension. But then, where else could it be?

A funny thing happened on the way to Filmport

In 2006, the Toronto Economic Development Corporation, the City's development arm (it has since been broken up into Build Toronto and Invest Toronto), brokered a deal with Rose Corp., owner of Toronto Film Studios, to operate the newly built waterside Filmport (now Pinewood Toronto Studios). The City neglected to do local planning studies in preparation for a redevelopment on Eastern Avenue, and when Rose Corp. prepared to move camp down to the water, it created a vacuum in Leslieville, which was at that time a mostly lower-income neighbourhood.

Developer SmartCentres suggested they'd fill the space with a mega-mall – likely Walmart. A coalition of residents and film workers sprang up in opposition. Pressed by the community, Councillor Paula Fletcher's office asked planning staff to reject the proposal. SmartCentres appealed. A complex fight at the Ontario Municipal Board ensued.

Community opposition moved in from many directions, but hinged on two points: loss of affordable studio space and the prospect of flooding an already struggling part of town with poorly paid jobs. The health of a community that had grown around art hinged not on new studio space, but on things with distinctly unartful-sounding names: zoning, employment land policies, 'avenue studies.'

The City won, and though many viewed the verdict as a victory City Hall earned on behalf of the community, one could also interpret it as the redemption of an often intangible and diffuse planning process by a community: a flagship arts development threatened to leave arts workers in the lurch. The Leslieville near-miss illustrates the fact that there's more to creative cities than creative infrastructure, and suggests that seeking to compete in a 'creative' economy has the potential to be downright destructive.

Rose Corp.'s loss in the Battle of Eastern Avenue drove them to quietly divest themselves of the new studio they helped build.

It was later renamed Pinewood Toronto Studios, after the British company that stepped in to fill the void – an unremarkable epilogue to Toronto's collective infrastructure fetish, the Cultural Renaissance.

The Cultural Renaissance is dead ...

Midway through the aughts, those two words – Cultural Renaissance, both straightforward enough on their own – began appearing everywhere together, signifying something unclear but ... big. In a way it seemed more like hopeful incantation than description, as if Toronto's urban tastemakers had gathered in the bathroom, turned off the light and begun repeating, 'Cultural Renaissance,' until it appeared in the mirror.

In April 2007, I ... signed up ... or ... (insert verb here: registered? asked? applied? prayed?) for Google Alerts, emails that are generated each time a certain phrase is indexed, for the words 'Toronto' and 'Cultural Renaissance,' and one arrived cheerily every couple of days until 2009, when the term began to subtly fall from fashion. People weren't using it as often by then, and those who did seemed less and less clear on what – or where – the Cultural Renaissance was. It had gone missing. I sensed foul play.

Testimonies of those who'd seen it last gave rise to an interesting possibility. We know it had expensive tastes: '[A] billion-dollar cultural renaissance,'[1] 'Unprecedented capital investment';[2] and we're pretty sure it was last located downtown ('Bloor Street West, in the heart of Toronto's designated cultural renaissance,'[3] 'thriving downtown area ... driving the city's ongoing cultural renaissance'[4]).

1 travel.nationalgeographic.co.uk/travel/city-guides/toronto-canada/
2 Canadian Actors' Equity Association submission on the 2010 provincial budget.
3 cgi.ebay.co.uk/Holiday-Inn-Toronto-Midtown,-Toronto,-Canada_W0QQitemZ3204
86641718QQcmdZViewItemQQimsxq20100212?IMSfp=TL1002121210001r20106
4 www.lostateminor.com/2009/06/04/torontos-luminato/

So, what's big, expensive and located downtown? Buildings. Witnesses to Renaissance activity, speaking almost exclusively of buildings, seemed to confirm the assumption: the Cultural Renaissance had become a building and had probably met its end at the hands of one, too. Seven stood to gain: the Toronto International Film Festival's Bell Lightbox, the Royal Conservatory of Music's Telus Centre, the Gardiner Museum, the Royal Ontario Museum's Michael Lee-Chin Crystal, the Art Gallery of Ontario, the Four Seasons Centre for the Performing Arts and the National Ballet School.

Thanks, ironically, to a legacy of former Conservative premier Mike Harris's provincial SuperBuild fund, they all had the means. And though the Bell Lightbox may have arranged, as architecture critic Alex Bozikovic (somewhat menacingly) put it, the Renaissance's 'finale,' two separate sources agreed that the Telus Centre made off with the 'crown jewel.' And, being on Bloor West, had penetrated the 'heart' of the Renaissance to do it.

I flip over my cards and end the game: it was Telus, on Bloor Street, with the Royal Conservatory of Music. The loot has been divvied up, and it seems no one wishes to speak further of the sordid affair. The Cultural Renaissance is dead.

... Long live the cultural renaissance

'You don't have to build an opera house,' says Che Kothari. 'You can walk down to the corner and see a freestyle session going on. That is the heart and soul of the renaissance that I'm a part of.'

Kothari is founder of Manifesto Community Projects. It's a network uniting artists and musicians across the city and across disciplines, drawing heavily from the hip-hop scene. It has also recently emerged as a potential political force at City Hall.

'Going out to a community centre and watching b-boys practice – that is the renaissance. A group like Lost Lyrics teaching through hip-hop culture in Malvern, or the LIFE Movement guys sitting in an apartment at Jane and Finch, planning to bring KRS-One down [to speak at a town hall meeting]. That's the renaissance. It's happening on all levels.'

For now, though, it may be happening faster on the first level – that is, what David Hulchanski called the 'First Toronto.' In 'The Three Cities Within Toronto,' a groundbreaking 2007 study sponsored by the University of Toronto's Centre for Urban and Community Studies, Hulchanski found that Toronto is made up of three economically and geographically discrete cities: the inner core, where prosperity has been increasing; the centre ring, where it has remained more or less stable; and the outer ring, where the average income is falling steadily. People in the core tend to be pale-skinned. Those in the outer ring don't. The outer ring has also tended, in the last fifty years, to be the site of most of our industrial base, now dwindling.[5]

In the parlance of economic development, the 'Creative City' seems to often function as a half-acknowledged euphemism for Post-Industrial City That Hasn't Ended Up Like the Set of Thunderdome. Richard Florida's dogged work to privilege creativity as an economic force has relied in large part on horror stories of industrial wrecks too slow to change course. These bogeyman city stories – which, like all enduring bogeymen, are rooted in truth – have certainly been a boon for serious artists looking to be treated like grown-ups by civic structures, but may also help lubricate the very process from which they purport to steer us.

'Working-class regions possess among the lowest levels of human capital,' writes Florida in *The Rise of the Creative Class*; for any city not reborn as a creative centre, 'the economic and social future is troubling.' While he does urge us to 'be more imaginative in finding ways to make service, and even manufacturing,

5 The flight of industrial capital, nothing new for North American cities, is tied to a number of factors. many out of any municipality's control. But does it happen entirely in isolation of municipal policies, especially those crafted in pursuit of the 'Creative City'?

jobs more creative,' the message, supported by pages of figures, rings clear: industry is an albatross around our collective neck.

But can the Third Toronto survive the loss of industry? Has it so far? For those able to safely jump ship to the new 'creative' economy, yes. But for the majority shut out of 'Creative' work, there is increasingly only one other option: the story of dead-end service jobs against which Leslieville fought so hard at the Ontario Municipal Board.

We usually neglect to invoke Coleridge's poem in full. That albatross was only bad luck once someone went and killed it.

Shifting focus

'People will express themselves,' says Adonis Huggins, program director for Regent Park Focus. 'That need will always be there, even if it's repressed. And sometimes it comes out negatively. I don't think that's necessarily a class thing. But there is that question, that question of potential: "Is there more? Isn't there anywhere else I can go?"'

Working from a reclaimed basement in the Toronto Community Housing neighbourhood that is its namesake, Focus evolved from an unprecedented process: in 1990, Ontario's Anti-Drug Secretariat dispensed millions of dollars in funding to 'communities vulnerable to drug abuse.' Those communities determined their needs and designed their programs, including Regent Park Focus, which soon grew into a bootstrap media production company.

Regent Park is a diverse community, but Huggins found he was hearing a common note from neighbourhood youth. They were angered by news media portrayal of their sometimes troubled but tightly knit area. Broadcasts only ever seemed to mention the neighbourhood like some sort of prefix to violence. He started restructuring the program as a multimedia workshop, with the goal of training kids to produce their own news reports.

'You can get them involved in sports, you can get them out to dances – if you say, "We're going to talk about issues that are affecting the community," they're gone,' he tells me with a laugh. 'But this means something to them. This is when we started having more youth than adults [in the program].'

Adonis Huggins

When (or if) governing structures attempt to tackle the effects of economic inequality, art is usually placed very low on a very long existential-to-do list, thanks to being so high up in Old Man Maslow's hierarchy. But in Huggins' description of his work, art is a necessity at every level, suffusing and uniting the practical and the spiritual.

'[Media arts work] gives them a sense of "Wow, I can do this? You mean I could go to school for journalism? Or I could do photography for a living?"' Through art, participants see a potential solution to the hierarchies – both Maslow's and the economy's – above them: lateral thinking. Go artsy. In a computer lab in the basement of a marginalized community, the next generation imagines itself able to quite literally adjust the margins. 'We're doing public health work,' says Huggins. 'They are producing art about the stresses in their lives.'

'The journal of a sea animal living on land'
– Carl Sandburg, on poetry

If art can form a practical base for (or suggest an alternative to) life's pyramid, if building a new film studio can be bad for a film community and if a founder of the marquee Manifesto festival can, speaking of the cultural renaissance, speak quite literally of pedestrian things – street corners and community centres – then maybe I can be forgiven for suggesting that one of the most creative places in a city is the public pool.

I'm a swimmer. To swimmers, swimming is serious business, but it's hard to imagine a more absurd task. Having put on my special magic short pants, I plunge into an enormous, carefully engineered puddle, and travel back and forth until, having spent an hour going nowhere, I emerge from the humid pit at the same point at which I entered, exhausted, and take a shower to wash away the water.

It's also hard to imagine a better analogy for the artistic process: the pool serves the same function as the empty page, stage or canvas, a space for the body to keep busy while the mind (spirit, subconscious, muse – name your swim coach) sneaks off to figure itself out. At the end of their work, both swimmer and artist have gone nowhere, and that's the point: their travels were internal.

It was public pools, not schools, where I began to understand Auden's insistence that 'Poetry makes nothing happen' (or Camus' suggestion that 'One must imagine Sisyphus happy').

The pool has answered questions about unfinished poems and unhealthy relationships. It's helped me make first pitches and find final paragraphs. It has allowed me that greatest luxury ever afforded an artist: time and space to do something that serves no demonstrable purpose (including, especially, distraction). Space in which to move freely, just for free movement's sake.

There are more obvious benefits. I feel smarter and more alert when I've been exercising. And the rec-centre change room is an equalizer where people from varying backgrounds commingle: working-class second-generation Portuguese youth; a new immigrant from Jamaica; a police constable. And none, for a brief time, has power over another. (It's hard to feel entitled when you're scuttling around in a towel.)

Now substitute for the pool whatever feels more relevant: ball court, bike lane, library. Could we have any vibrant arts scene without public transit? Whatever allows you space to move facilitates space to connect with yourself and others, especially the selves and others you wouldn't have known to seek out otherwise.

In contrast to a theorized, individualized 'creative class' of people, we might consider the shared attributes of an existing class of amenities, something I'll call 'conducive infrastructure.' Just as the participants of Regent Park Focus discovered the foundational nature of arts, the idea of conducive infrastructure suggests the ecstatic potential present in the mundane consistency of any foundational city services like parks and rec centres. The idea of conducive infrastructure may also present a possible strategy for straddling sometimes stifling distinctions between the public and private sectors, but without eroding necessary safety barriers between them. The rec centre finds its analogues in meeting spaces like small local coffee bars, restaurants, bookshops, video stores, grocers, clubs and theatres.

And suffice to say for now that conducive infrastructure is most possible where the most people are. Of course, art can be made in any architectural context. We have an artistic archetype(/stereotype) for just about every built form: cabin-bound poet, suburban b-boy, west-side indie rocker, derelict industrial-loft–living painter. But fine-grain urban density increases the opportunity for self-directed, unplanned encounters, collaboration and cross-pollination.

But where this desirability also drives rising rents, the benefits may be too often pyrrhic. Cultural capital may save some from the first wave of exile, but how many will be spared, in the end, from their own success as urban terraformers?

Ruby, Ruby, Ruby Soho

Tim Jones, CEO of non-profit developer Artscape, refers to the consequences of Hulchanski's findings as the 'SoHo effect,' a nod to the once bohemian, now bougie Manhattan district. He doesn't believe, however, that the effect is inevitable. And that belief is what part of what drives Artscape. We talk it over in one of the big-windowed meeting rooms at their offices in Liberty Village, the 'rejuvenated' former industrial district just southeast of Parkdale.

'The story is always told as the same sad lament that casts artists as the hapless victims of this process,' says Jones. 'I think telling that story in that way is part of our problem.' His formula is simple. 'If value is being generated [by artists],' he says, 'surely there's a way to capture it and reinvest it in the health and interests of the creative community.'

Artscape's first major success was the founding of the Distillery District. The tony development is hardly class-neutral; the first real test of the Artscape approach may have been the case of the high-rise with the risible name, the Bohemian Embassy that now looms over the mouth of West Queen West.

Community opposition to the towers was squashed at the Ontario Municipal Board, owing, by some accounts, to an over-whelmed community planning apparatus and a political system too slow to react. Dashed too was a City plan to impose a quota for affordable units in the building. Enter Artscape. Acting as a sort of sub-developer, the company purchased seventy units from the tower's developer at cost, then convinced planners to grant the developer more height and density. Forty-eight units will be sold through an affordable home-ownership program, the profit being used to subsidize the remaining twenty-two as affordable rental units. 'The city just gave up air to create affordable housing,' says Jones. 'It wasn't steeped in the usual red tape.'

Artscape's intervention on West Queen West happened in the context of a flawed, if not outright subverted, community planning process. And in the end, it will likely only serve to partially mitigate, rather than to slow – let alone reverse – the economic homogenization of Queen West.

Yet Artscape's success suggests a rupture in the traditional narrative in which neither market nor government forces have been willing (the former) or able (the latter) to retell the story, as Jones says, of artists and urbanity. It implies, as well, future possibilities for commercial spaces.[6] Affordable housing in one step. Affordable galleries might be the next.

The kids are all right

There's no charge to hang out in the public gallery of City Council chambers, of course. But Devon Ostrom still isn't sure it's worth the cost.

'I've got a Master's in curation,' he says. 'When your whole job is producing bullshit, you're good at sniffing it out.' He laughs. He's joking. Maybe.

Sharing a booth in the bright and empty cafeteria of City Hall, we talk about the eight years he spent navigating City decision-making structures, bringing to fruition (a mitigated failure by his standards, and an unprecedented success-in-progress by those of many insiders) a simple but beautiful bastard brainchild: a tax on billboards.

The concept behind the Beautiful City Billboard Fee was simple from the start: levy a modest tax on billboards and put it towards arts funding. It seemed like a no-brainer, as they say in the art world. Governments tax things, and the government

6 Ever noticed how newer towers usually grow out of corporate franchises? Developers tend to have a hard time selling main-floor units as residential spaces, so it's 'better' to get franchisees who can afford to take a large section off their hands all at once. If city planners were empowered to dictate the maximum area ('floorplate') of units for even a portion of the first couple of floors (or 'podium') of a new tower, and an interested organization was able to implement a commercial version of the Artscape model, independent merchants could be given a new level of access to urban development.

in question, led by a thin majority of David Miller supporters, certainly seemed to dig on art.

But when we speak, in March 2010, Ostrom is exhausted, and ready to hand over the reins. 'City Hall wasn't designed to be fertile ground,' he says. 'It's barren. It takes an inordinate amount of effort. There are some serious problems with the way that the City deals with citizen-led initiatives, and that's something which requires a lot of thought at the City.'

Insert a pithy rumination on the relationship between volume of darkness and proximity of dawn: since our chat, the tax's existence was approved, and BeautifulCity.ca, an alliance of Manifesto (with which Ostrom also works) and some of the city's public-space activists secured slim political support for a portion of the money to be directed to the arts-funding envelope.

It's an interesting study in how a simple proposal blossomed – or mutated – into a series of discrete but overlapping struggles. But it's also not what the alliance of mostly young activists was promised: 100 per cent of the tax revenues were supposed to go to the arts. In 2010, a portion went towards creating and staffing the enforcement regime, and even that was hard-won. As this book goes to print in October 2010, the three remaining news-media-anointed mayoral candidates have all promised to devote the money towards arts funding over their first term.

Whatever the outcome, the coalition stands as something of a miracle: dozens and dozens of youth, many from outside the core, poured their spirits into a City Hall often perceived to waver between indifference and hostility. But doggedness knitted a loose network of young artists and arts workers into a constituency that Council had to respect and even court. Informal jam sessions organized by the activists and attended by influential councillors – some of them members of the budget committee – did more to illuminate the political process than the entire press corps did in the eight years since Ostrom first proposed the tax.

The art and the possible

Adam Vaughan was one such councillor. In the spring of 2010, I asked him what lessons artists and activists could take from Beautiful City.

The most important lesson, he says, is to always expand your circle of allies. A stranger's just a friend you haven't engaged in political horse-trading with yet.

'They've just [pushed] back at Shelley [Carroll, budget chief], at Gord [Perks], at me, when they should [have been finding] the next four people on the right wing to convince,' he says. 'If the space was actually there for [the budget committee] to do it, they'd be the first to champion the arts. It's one thing to create the space for a policy debate, and another to create the space to deliver the policy.'

And that is about political power. 'Create the political conditions such that it's possible. Get people elected ... Get seats on boards. Then you can start to decode [the system], and you can decode it for your constituencies.'

He points to cycling as an example. 'It went from a movement, to policy, to a social dynamic that is now directing how we do sidewalk repair and urban design. It's gone from a quirky thing to a way to deliver services,' says Vaughan. In his mind, the best example of this kind of activism is still the 1970s movement against the Spadina Expressway. 'The movement wasn't just about Spadina. It was about taking over Council. It was about how we use power.'

Politics, then, shares at least one imperative with art: clear yourself enough space to work. And among those with whom I spoke, there arose other common threads that support the analogy between politics to artistic process. This is my arrangement. Cut and paste, scratch and sniff, mix and remix as you please.

Create your own forms

There may be, for better or worse, a new stratum of governance bodies arising – non-governmental, but closer to the inside than NGOs. I mention this to Tim Jones. 'Connector organizations,' he says with a nod, adding the Centre for Social Innovation as another example. Find them.

Or, finding none that serve your community's needs, make them. Manifesto did. 'The best movements are cross-sectoral,' says Che Kothari. 'Arts play a role in economic development, youth engagement, social justice, violence reduction, health. Around the [Beautiful City Billboard Fee] table, we should have had education, legal – all different sectors talking about the importance of arts funding. And when other issues are on the table, arts people should show up there as well.'

Learn from other disciplines

'Grassroots cats know how to use funding,' says Kothari with a knowing laugh. 'We can get a lot of things done for a lot less ... But through our experience working with the Royal Ontario Museum, with Luminato, these huge institutions, we've started to implement some systems we might not have thought of.'

'Art is food. You can't eat it but it feeds you.'
– Bread and Puppet Theatre, Cheap Art Manifesto

'The [Wychwood Barns] had been sitting there for thirty years,' says Jones of another Artscape development. 'The community had lots of ideas but no one figured out how to make it happen. It was about working through a sometimes painful community process ... to grow a groundswell of support. We purposefully looked beyond just serving artists. We asked, "How can this serve the community?" And people were far more willing to have conversations with us.'

People in the system have their own political struggles as well. Do yours overlap? 'A relationship with staff is the most important relationship you'll have at City Hall,' says Ostrom. 'It takes a lot of respect, a lot of reciprocation and a lot of trust. One of the things we did was start actively advocating for [BCBF] money to go towards enhanced enforcement, towards the needed staff [level].'

Writing happens in the editing

'And always watch where the documents are going, rather than what Council is saying,' Ostrom adds. 'The agendas, the decision [documents]. Disregard PowerPoints, look at appendices ... That was painful to learn. No matter how much political pressure we applied, something was out of alignment. So I went back through documents, which brought me back to November, where the word "offset" was first swapped in for "enhance." You can see a motivation, or an interest, when you see an anomaly.'

'If your life is burning well, [art] is just the ash' – Leonard Cohen

Arts activists should remember not to focus all their energy on City Hall. Everything done to make the city more artful, to make art present in and integral to city life can only create more political space.

Camilla Holland is general manager at Tarragon Theatre and a co-chair of ArtsVote. 'It's hard to convince someone of [the political value of art] until they see the intrinsic value of art. Even if I can convince [a right-wing councillor] of the economic impact, he would still feel it's wrong for us to be in the public purse. We're going to have to connect with kids, with schools. We have to say, "Okay, there's no arts organization in your ward, but look at all the arts work being done in your rec centres." These are anchor organizations. They are providing such service for such value. The arts provide service that the market just couldn't bear.' Or, at least, wouldn't.

'It's groundwork,' says Kothari. 'Being tight. We brought together people who were already doing things, and decided to work towards a festival and town-hall meetings … And now there's a desire from councillors to see that energy at City Hall on a regular basis. And we did it in a way that made people feel comfortable to sit in one of those seats [at City Hall]. They walk into the space, and say, "Oh, there's music, I've heard this music, there are people in these seats that look like me, that feel like me." When we start, we say, "By the way, this is a public space – you are meant to be here …" It's an unravelling. It's having the right people doing the work. People who can bridge that space.'

And what, if not that, do artists do?

The creative city exists, but for now it sits empty. Its future citizens still work too hard for others' ends to explore their own and claim their space: space for connections to be made, for the mind to wander free from industry, exhaustion, debt, distraction. Space, as poet Don McKay says, 'where we can sit … exhilarated and heartbroken.' Why, if not for that, build cities?

Get involved

themanifesto.ca

catchdaflava.com

torontoartscape.on.ca

beautifulcity.ca

Spoken word artist, language arts educator, City Hall columnist, campaign press secretary, rumoured 'secret weapon' of the Macedonian Liberation Army during the 1940s: **Mike Smith** has been many things, most of them ill-advised, all of them delicious, and only one of them affecting the space-time continuum in any serious way. Try to guess which one! Then check linebreaks.com for the answer – you may be surprised.

About the editors

Dave Meslin is a Toronto-based artist and organizer who has instigated a variety of urban projects, including Reclaim the Streets, the Toronto Public Space Committee, *Spacing* magazine, City Idol, Human River, Toronto Cyclists Union, the WindFest Kite Festival, *Dandyhorse* magazine and the Ranked Ballot Initiative. When he's not deeply immersed in urban politics or electoral reform, Dave tours with local pop band the Hidden Cameras. Multipartisan and fiercely optimistic, Dave embraces ideas and projects that cut across traditional boundaries between grassroots politics, electoral politics and the arts community.

Christina Palassio is the co-editor of several books in the *uTOpia* series, including *HtO: Toronto's Water from Lake Iroquois to Lost Rivers to Low-flow Toilets* and *The Edible City: Toronto's Food from Farm to Fork*. She has also written for the *Globe and Mail*, the *Montreal Gazette* and *Matrix* magazine, and is the books columnist for *THIS Magazine*.

Alana Wilcox is the Editorial Director of Coach House Books. She is one of the founding editors of the *uTOpia* series, and an editor of *uTOpia*, *The State of the Arts*, *GreenTOpia* and *The Edible City*. She is also the author of a novel, *A Grammar of Endings*.

Typeset in Benton Sans and Whitman
Printed and bound at the Coach House on bpNichol Lane, November 2010

Cover drawing and design by Jason Logan
Interior design by Alana Wilcox
Photo of John Sewell, p. 17, by Liz Rykert
Photo of Devon Ostrom, p. 64, by Tyler Young
Photo of Alejandra Bravo, p. 139, by Gregory Bennett
All other photos by Matt O'Sullivan

Coach House Books
80 bpNichol Lane
Toronto ON M5S 3J4

416 979 2217
800 367 6360

mail@chbooks.com
www.chbooks.com